W9-BRI-867

TETON TRAILS

A GUIDE TO THE TRAILS OF GRAND TETON NATIONAL PARK

by Katy Duffy and Darwin Wile

Published by the
Grand Teton Natural History Association

In Cooperation with the
NATIONAL PARK SERVICE, U.S. DEPARTMENT OF THE INTERIOR

Cover Photograph by Frederic Joy, Light Reflections

Scratchboard Drawings by Bryan Harry

Inside Front and Inside Back Cover Art by Grant Hagen

Line Drawings by NPS staff

Geological Illustrations by Jennifer Ziegler

© 1995 Text by Katy Duffy and Darwin Wile

Project Coordination by Sharlene Milligan

Published by Grand Teton Natural History Association

Book Design, Typography and Production by Sherry West

Text Editing by Just Write

Lithography by Patterson Printing

First Printing 1995

ISBN 0-931895-35-9

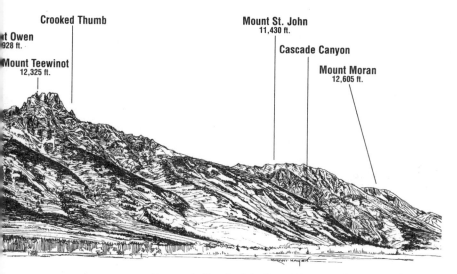

NORTH→

Crooked Thumb

Mount St. John
11,430 ft.

t Owen
928 ft.

Mount Teewinot
12,325 ft.

Cascade Canyon

Mount Moran
12,605 ft.

Panoramic Sketch of the Teton Mountains by Grant Hagen

Dedicated to everyone who loves the natural world.
If a soaring bird takes your breath away,
if a flower brings you to your knees,
if you ponder the mystery of the rocks,
if you're at home in the woods, or yearn to be,
then this book's for you.
Welcome to Teton Trails!
DW

CONTENTS

MAPS

FOREWORD

An invitation...
Man's welfare and his existence are but reflections of the quality of his environment.

Today, there appears to be a nationwide awakening to this fundamental truth. Americans in our day of mechanization, industrial complexes, and sprawling cities, are increasingly aware of the urgency for protecting our natural environment.

Unspoiled natural environment is exemplified in our national parks. It is in these special places where we discover the intricate interrelationships among the elements involved; the fragile nature of the environment; and hopefully how man can live in harmony in the natural community.

There is no better way to gain understanding and appreciation than to don hiking clothes and take to the trails. The smell of pine, the song of a bird, the color of a flower, all add to the joy of an invigorating hike.

Across flower-filled meadows, along the shores of placid lakes, beside turbulent mountain streams, or among lofty peaks; more than 200 miles of well-maintained trails thread their way through the park.

For a truly recreational experience; leave the comfort of your car; yield to the lure of Teton Trails.

From Teton Trails, by Bryan Harry, 1961

Bryan Harry served as Assistant Chief Naturalist in Grand Teton National Park from 1955-1968. One of Bryan's many accomplishments during his assignment here was to compile and complete the trail descriptions for a hiking guide to Grand Teton National Park. Bryan completed his task in 1961 and *Teton Trails* was professionally printed for the first time. From 1961 until 1995, Bryan's *Teton Trails* has been the bible for hiking information. It has been reprinted many times through the years, sporadically revised, and cosmetically changed to reflect more modern hiking equipment and improvements in photography.

The old classic on trails by Bryan Harry has been a good friend of mine and many millions of visitors to Grand Teton National Park. I have enjoyed hiking the trails he described so well and particularly liked his invitation to "yield to the lure of Teton Trails". Because Bryan's message of preserving and conserving is timeless, I have chosen to include it here in the foreword to our new edition so as not to lose all traces of it. Bryan's artistic talent also remains in the scratch board illustrations we have copied from the original booklet.

Bryan's exhortations to gain an understanding and appreciation of our natural environment are even more essential today and, certainly, part of my motivation to accept Darwin and Katy's idea to publish a new Teton Trails—offering a generous supply of natural history information to enhance trail descriptions. If you carry their expanded and updated version of *Teton Trails* with you into the mountains, you will be rewarded by the additional information which we hope will increase your awareness of the natural world and validate the reasons it must be protected.

Sharlene Milligan, Executive Director,
Grand Teton Natural History Association

Harebell

ACKNOWLEDGMENTS
Katy and Darwin want to thank several important people:
Patrick Matheny and Lynette Wile for being the perfect hiking
buddies; Bill Swift, Chief Naturalist of Grand Teton National Park,
for supporting this project; Backcountry ranger, Jay VanDerveer,
for guiding us through his backyard—Webb, Owl and Berry
canyons; Kristen Meckem, for pitching in at the last hour;
and special thanks to our birding pal, Bert Raynes.

INTRODUCTION
by Darwin Wile

I like hiking. But my hikes are far more than just walks. The distractions of the natural world have a way of turning my simple hikes from point A to point B into kaleidoscopic journeys filled with birds, mammals, wildflowers, and rocks. Sometimes it's enough just to sit down along the trail and observe what's going on around me. But often I have questions, the answers to many of which I don't know. What is that unfamiliar birdsong? Why did the vegetation along the trail change so abruptly? How did that enormous, solitary boulder find its way to the middle of the meadow? What insect made that tiny trail across the path?

It occurred to me on a trail one day that Grand Teton National Park should have a book designed for the hiker like me who is interested in more than just getting from point A to point B. This book would go beyond maps and mileages. Trail descriptions would give hints of the wildflowers, wildlife, and geology expected on each hike. Checklists of mammals, birds, wildflowers, and trees would be included to help in their identification. And sections on geology, habitats, animal behavior, and other useful information would be offered to help the hiker become more adept at reading the landscape and thereby better understanding the world of nature.

Katy Duffy is a naturalist at Grand Teton National Park. I met her through the Jackson Hole Bird Club. What I lacked in knowledge and credentials to write this book, Katy had in spades. I approached her with the idea and a proposal for co-authoring the book. We worked out the details and a few days later took the idea to Sharlene Milligan at Grand Teton Natural History Association. Sharlene liked the idea and, in that first meeting, came up with the title, *Teton Trails.*

Katy and I hiked virtually every mile of every trail in Grand Teton National Park. I asked her a million questions, noted her answers, and I learned so much. All the while, Sharlene looked over our shoulders and maintained our focus. It's fair and entirely accurate to say that *Teton Trails* is a product of all three of us.

We don't expect this book to answer all your questions on the trail. We do hope it will better prepare you intellectually and physically, make each hike more exciting and interesting, and help you feel more at home in the natural world.

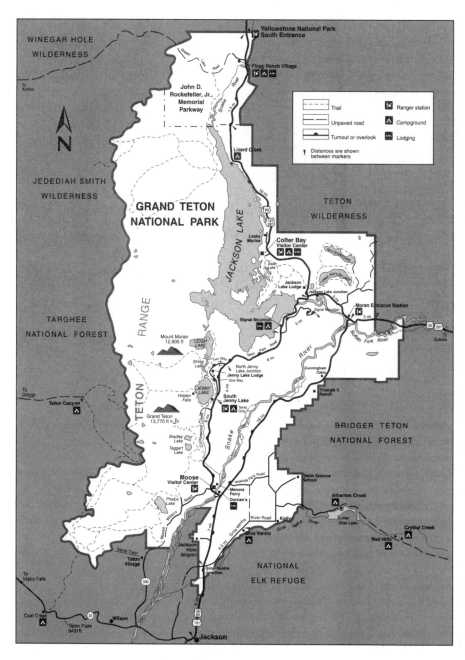

GRAND TETON NATIONAL PARK

PART I
PREPARATION

HELPFUL INFORMATION

BACKCOUNTRY HIKES

Explore glaciated canyons beneath towering pinnacles. Walk through meadows of wildflowers. Experience the Teton backcountry by taking a hike. Backcountry hikes can range from a few hours to a few days. Over 200 miles of trails await those with time, stamina, and an adventurous spirit.

Much of the following information has been gleaned from literature produced by Grand Teton National Park personnel. Hiking in the park will almost always be a safe, enjoyable experience for those who are prepared, who know and adhere to the park regulations, and who adopt a conservative attitude regarding their abilities and the possible dangers.

Plan your hikes well. Underestimating the time or distance involved can turn into a hike in the dark. At best, hiking in the dark is difficult and, at worst, it is dangerous. Most hikers average about 2 miles per hour on level trails, less on uphill trails. These averages do not include stops to rest and enjoy the surroundings.

CLOTHING

For day hikes, a small backpack will hold the necessities. Layering makes sense. Wear a T-shirt, long-sleeved shirt, and a wool sweater or synthetic pile jacket. Either shorts or long pants are appropriate in the summer. Take a hat with a sun visor and rain gear. That leaves enough space in your backpack for a water bottle, lunch, and extra clothes in case the weather changes. Hiking socks and good hiking boots (or sturdy running shoes) that fit well and have been broken in are a necessity.

For overnight camping, bring an extra shirt, long pants, and underwear. Wearing wet or sweat-soaked clothes to bed makes for a long, cold night. Much of the body's heat loss is from the head and feet. Bring a warm hat, an extra pair of wool socks to wear to bed, and a pair of gloves or mittens. For wilderness camping, bring a pair of stream-crossing shoes—old sneakers, rubber sandals, or boat shoes.

EQUIPMENT

For day hikes of less than 10 miles, usually 1 quart of water is enough. For day hikes over 10 miles, bring more water or carry a filtering system. Do not drink the water from the lakes and streams (see **Water**, page 6). A first aid kit, moleskin for blisters, sunscreen, lip balm, sunglasses with UV protection, toilet paper and a plastic bag, insect repellent, a compass and a topographic trail map (sold at visitor centers), a versatile (Swiss Army-type) knife, waterproof matches, and, of course, a lunch are all good ideas to include in a backpack. A pair of binoculars will often provide better views and help you find wildlife. A magnifying lens is useful for identifying and enjoying wildflowers. Field guides for birds, mammals, and wildflowers might also be desirable.

Much more equipment is needed for overnight hikes than for day hikes. Camping and hiking stores can be very helpful in recommending what quality and features to look for in camping equipment. Basic equipment should include a sleeping bag suitable for mountain camping, a light tent with ground cloth, sleeping pad, dried or lightweight food, strong nylon rope (50 feet) to hang food, a cooking stove and utensils, flashlight, and personal identification.

CAMPING

All overnight backcountry use requires a permit which can be obtained free at the Moose Visitor Center year-round or at the Jenny Lake Ranger Station and Colter Bay Visitor Center in the summer. With a permit, backcountry camping is allowed in a camping zone or lakeshore site for two consecutive nights. On Jackson Lake the limit is three nights. Groups (seven or more; twelve people maximum) must camp in designated group campsites. The backcountry camping limit is a total of ten nights parkwide between June 1 and September 15.

Thirty percent of backcountry camping sites in trailed canyons and all group campsites may be reserved; the rest are issued on a first-come, first-served basis. Make requests for reservations in writing between January 1 and May 15. Submit a final itinerary, including dates, each night's campsites, and the number of people in your party. Also include a second-choice itinerary and a telephone number. Mail requests to Permits Office, Grand Teton National Park, P.O. Box 170, Moose, WY 83012. Reserved permits must be picked up in person by 10:00 a.m. on the first day of the trip.

CAMPING ZONES—The backcountry of the Teton Range above 7,000 feet is divided into camping zones. Quotas for camping zones are based on the number of suitable campsites as well as campers' need for solitude. With a permit, you can stay anywhere within a designated camping zone. In trailed canyons, try to camp in previously used campsites. Camp at least 100 feet from lakes and streams. Park regulations prohibit fires in the backcountry, so bring a lightweight backpacking stove.

DESIGNATED SITES—Jackson, Bearpaw, Trapper, Leigh, and Phelps lakes have designated camping sites, and permits are required. Depending on fire conditions, campfires may be allowed in fire grates at these sites. Groups of seven to twelve must camp in designated group sites.

ELEVATION

The valley lies above 6,000 feet. Many of the trailheads are at 6,800 feet or higher. The tree line occurs at about 10,000 feet. Hiking in thin air feels very different from hiking at sea level. Taking a few days to acclimatize by taking short walks makes sense before embarking on more strenuous hikes. When you do begin longer periods of exercise, walk slowly, stop often, and drink a lot of water. You'll feel better and see more of the area.

DIFFICULTY OF TERRAIN

Hikes in Grand Teton National Park range in difficulty from an easy walk to a "technical" climb of one of the peaks (using ropes and other climbing equipment). Most of the hikes described in this guide require no more skill than the ability to walk on a trail.

Each hike is classified as *easy* (a walk), *moderate* (some hills), or *difficult* (steep hills and/or long distance). Almost anybody who can walk 5 to10 miles on flat terrain will be able to handle the *easy* hikes. *Moderate* hikes require the ability to walk 10 miles or more and to walk uphill for about a mile or for approximately 30 minutes. To enjoy a *difficult* hike requires a higher fitness level resulting from regular workouts and the ability to walk slowly but steadily uphill for at least 2 hours with only a few short breaks.

Most of the trails described in this guide are maintained and reasonably well-marked. When dry, trails usually afford good footing. When wet, any of the trails can be slippery and, in some cases, dangerous.

WATER

Cool, crystal-clear stream water looks tempting to drink. But be aware that as more people have camped and hiked in the backcountry, the incidence of intestinal infection from drinking untreated water has increased throughout the West. *Giardia lamblia, Campylobacter,* and other harmful bacteria may be transmitted through untreated water. Giardia is spread through the feces of contaminated mammals, including beaver, moose, elk, deer, and people.

When hiking, carry sufficient water from approved sources, such as water spigots and drinking fountains in the park. If water is used from lakes or streams, it must be boiled for a full minute in order to kill harmful organisms, or you can use a properly working filtration system. In a true emergency, find a spring or seep coming from deep in the mountain and take water from where it emerges.

Do not eat "watermelon snow"—that is, snow found early in the summer on north-facing slopes that has a pink color. This coloration is caused by algae growing in the snow. In the mountains, no water or snow should be consumed without filtering or boiling.

SANITATION

To prevent contamination of waterways, bury feces in a hole 6 to 8 inches deep at least 200 feet from streams or lakes. Pack out used toilet paper, tampons, sanitary napkins, and diapers in sealed plastic bags. Do not bury or burn them. Used toilet paper left along the trail is unsightly and reflects a poor backcountry ethic.

HUMAN NUISANCES

Grand Teton National Park hosts few natural "pests"—no poisonous snakes, chiggers, or fleas. Poison ivy grows in only one location (on the west side of Jackson Lake). Rabies cases have rarely been reported.

To ward off annoying mosquitoes and biting flies, or ticks in the spring, carry insect repellent. Lyme disease has not been reported in the park.

PRECAUTIONS AND SUGGESTIONS

Hikers in Grand Teton National Park will have a more pleasant experience if they follow these guidelines.

- Don't hike alone.
- Don't hike after dark.
- Avoid snowfields and glaciers. Without training and proper use of equipment, hiking or climbing on snow or ice is very dangerous.

- Only experienced climbers should attempt rock climbing.
- Be "bear aware". Avoid areas where there are dead animals. Bears are very possessive of carrion they have killed or found.
- Be careful in areas where berries are ripe. Bears love to eat berries and can be hidden by dense foliage.
- Know your location at all times. When confused or lost, immediately retrace your steps to your last position of certainty.
- Stay on established trails and hike single file.
- Avoid open areas and caves when there is lightning. It is safer in the forest during a thunderstorm.
- When walking down a steep hill, keep weight forward and downhill so feet are less likely to slide. Land each step on toes rather than heel. This cushions the shock to legs and joints.
- When walking up a steep hill, use a lock step. On each step, briefly lock your knee (without hyperextending your leg backward). This takes the strain off leg muscles and gives them a rest by putting the weight on your skeletal structure. Remember that small steps put less strain on muscles than large steps.
- Hiking etiquette dictates that the right-of-way always be yielded:
  1. To the hiker with the heavier burden;
  2. To the downhill hiker;
  3. To the faster hiker coming from the rear;
  4. To horses.

BACKCOUNTRY REGULATIONS

These "do's and don'ts" must be followed while inside the park:

- Pets, weapons, bicycles, or vehicles are not allowed on trails or in the backcountry.
- All overnight camping requires a free permit.
- Carry out all garbage.
- Hike on established trails to prevent erosion.
- Horses have the right-of-way. Step off the trail and remain quiet while horses pass.
- Respect wildlife. Observe and photograph from a safe distance. Do not approach or feed animals. Natural food assures their health and survival; staying a safe distance assures yours.

- Nesting birds of all species are easily disturbed.
  If an adult on a nest flies off, circles above, screams in
  alarm, or attacks, the nest has been approached too closely.
  You should leave the area immediately.

- Do not pick or disturb any vegetation in the park.
  One exception is that edible berries, plants, and mushrooms
  may be gathered for personal consumption, but be certain
  of their identification before eating any wild plants.

- Do not collect rocks, antlers, or bones.

LEAVE NO TRACE!

Hikers and campers should be aware of and follow minimum impact
hiking and camping practices.

- In high use areas, stay on established trails and camp in
  designated or previously used sites. Do nothing that will
  further impact trails and sites.

- In pristine areas where there are no established trails and
  campsites, try to walk and camp on rock, sand and other
  stable, non-vegetated surfaces. Avoid areas of fragile
  vegetation.

- When hiking and camping, minimize your impact on wildlife
  and other people in the area.

- Leave a campsite in a condition where even the most
  vigilant would not be aware you had been there.

- Do not bury or burn trash, litter and garbage. Pack it out!

- Try not to use soap when washing yourself or dishes.
  If you must use soap, wash with a biodegradable variety
  200 feet from the nearest water source, carrying a bucket
  of water to rinse yourself.

- Leave all natural objects where they are (wildflowers,
  antlers, driftwood, rocks, fossils, shells, etc.)

- Where fire grates and campfires are permitted, gather
  firewood from a large area at least 400 yards from your
  campsite. Use branches (no thicker than your wrist) from
  dead trees lying on the ground.

CLIMATE

A semi-arid climate contributes less than 20 inches of precipitation
annually to Jackson Hole. A good percentage of that precipitation

comes in the form of snow. Uncompromising winter reigns from December through March, and several feet of snow blanket the valley. The mountains lie buried under 10 to 20 feet. Daytime temperatures average in the 20s and 30s, while most nights find the mercury falling well below zero. The Moose Visitor Center distributes a map of marked ski trails, along with information on weather, avalanche, and road conditions.

Short and unpredictable springs arrive in the valley in April and May, melting snow and often bringing rain. As the snow recedes up the mountainsides, wildflowers emerge and cover the meadows. Valley temperatures average in the 50s and 60s during the day, and in the 20s and 30s at night. Snow usually melts off valley trails in May, but lingers in the mountains through much of the summer.

Summers nurture the valley from June through early September. Usually the sun shines continuously, occasionally interrupted by scattered afternoon thundershowers. Temperatures rise into the 70s and low 80s in the day, cooling down to the 40s and 50s at night. Mountain temperatures average 10 degrees cooler.

September and October can be special. Snow may cover the high mountains, while sun continues to shine in the valley. Autumn colors usually reach their peak in mid- to late September. Daytime temperatures stay in the 50s and 60s while the mercury sinks into the teens and 20s at night. November can be as lovely as October or as wintry as December.

Whatever time of year it is in Jackson Hole—be prepared! Mountains make it difficult to predict weather. Storms develop suddenly. Snow can fall anytime, especially at the higher elevations, and there is no month in which the valley is certain to be frost free. Snow conditions vary from year to year. Check at a visitor center for up-to-date information.

Summer's warm, sunny days and cool evenings can change quickly. Frequent afternoon thunderstorms occur during July and August. Cooler weather and less crowded conditions make September and October a good time for hiking, but nighttime temperatures may dip below freezing.

At any time of year, hypothermia (exposure sickness) can overcome a hiker soaked by a cold mountain storm. Always carry a wool or polypropylene sweater, jacket, and rain gear.

Warning signs of hypothermia include uncontrollable shivering, incoherent speech, and apparent exhaustion. Help the victim immediately. For mild cases, give the individual warm, nonalcoholic liquids and dry clothes. For serious cases, keep the patient awake, warm, and dry. Put the individual, stripped of cold, wet clothes, in a sleeping bag with another person and have the victim drink warm liquids.

At these elevations, an appropriate sunscreen and sunglasses are essential. The table below will assist in planning for the months of highest visitation.

	May	Jun	Jul	Aug	Sep
Average High Temperature (°F)	61	71	81	79	69
Average Low Temperature (°F)	31	37	41	39	32
Average Rainfall (Inches)	3	2	1	1	1

OTHER ACTIVITIES

The park offers the following outdoor activities.

HUNTING—Hunting is not permitted in Grand Teton National Park with one exception: each fall a special drawing is held for an elk reduction program. Anyone planning to hike in the park after September 15 should check with a ranger to see when and where the hunt is being held. It is best not to hike in hunting areas. Anyone planning to be in or near a hunting area should wear a blaze orange vest.

FISHING—Anglers may test their skills by trying to catch whitefish and cutthroat, lake, and brown trout in lakes and rivers of the park. Fishing conforms with Wyoming and National Park Service regulations. Obtain fishing regulations at the Moose, Jenny Lake, or Colter Bay visitor centers. A Wyoming fishing license, required for fishing in the park, may be purchased at the Moose Village Store, Signal Mountain Lodge, Colter Bay Marina, and Flagg Ranch Village. The Moose Visitor Center is open all year, while the other visitor centers are open only in the summer.

SWIMMING—Swimming is allowed in all lakes. None of the swimming areas has lifeguards. The Snake River is dangerous, and swimming in it is not recommended.

CLIMBING—Mountain climbing may be hazardous, even for the most experienced climbers. Registration is voluntary; overnight trips require a free backcountry permit. The Jenny Lake Ranger Station is the center for climbing information and registration from early June to mid-September. Obtain current weather information and route conditions. Ask the staff about proper equipment, route descriptions, and conditions. Solo climbs are not advised.

PARKWATCH

It is possible to play an important role in protecting and preserving Grand Teton National Park. Prevent, be alert to, and report hazards, accidents, fires, vandalism, and crime. Be aware of illegal activities such as hunting, poaching, and harassing wildlife. If someone breaks park rules or commits a crime, do not attempt to take action yourself. This is a job for a ranger. Discreetly note the location and descriptions of the people involved, and report the incident as soon as possible. If a phone is nearby, call 911 or Park Dispatch at 739-3301.

ORGANIZATIONS

Some organizations that may be useful before or during your visit to Grand Teton National Park are listed below with addresses and phone numbers.

GRAND TETON NATIONAL PARK
P.O. Box 170, Moose, WY 83012. (307) 739-3300.

GRAND TETON NATURAL HISTORY ASSOCIATION
P.O. Box 170, Moose, WY 83012. (307) 739-3606. This private, not-for-profit organization operates bookstores in visitor centers in the park and in Bridger-Teton and Targhee national forests. A mail-order catalog is available upon request.

NATIONAL ELK REFUGE
P.O. Box C, Jackson, WY 83001. (307) 733-9212. The refuge is best known as a winter range and feeding ground for about 9,000 elk. In winter, horse-drawn sleighs take visitors out among the elk herds. Refuge headquarters remains open all year from 8:00 a.m. to 4:30 p.m.

BRIDGER-TETON NATIONAL FOREST
P.O. Box 1888, Jackson, WY 83001. (307) 739-5500. The National Forest borders Jackson Hole on three sides. Recreational activities provided by the forest service include campgrounds, swimming, fishing, hunting, hiking, and boating. Skiing and snowmobiling are permitted in the winter.

TETON SCIENCE SCHOOL
P.O. Box 68, Kelly, WY 83011. (307) 733-4765. Located in Grand Teton National Park, the school offers courses in the natural sciences. Day and residential programs are included for young students and adults.

YELLOWSTONE NATIONAL PARK
P.O. Box 168, Yellowstone National Park, WY 82190. (307) 344-7381.
The nation's oldest national park, Yellowstone offers extensive services, including visitor centers, lodging, restaurants, and service stations.

CHAMBER OF COMMERCE
P.O. Box E, Jackson, WY 83001. (307) 733-3316.

Other Useful Telephone Numbers (307)

Emergency	911
Colter Bay Visitor Center	739-3594
Jenny Lake Visitor Center	739-3392
Teton County Sheriff (Assistance)	733-2331
Teton County Sheriff (Administration)	733-4052
Jackson Police	733-1430
Road Report	733-9966
Backcountry weather & avalanche forecast (winter only)	733-2664
Wyoming Game and Fish Department	733-2321

GEOLOGY OF JACKSON HOLE

Gaining an overview of the natural history of Grand Teton National Park requires some understanding of the geology of Jackson Hole. The landscape we see today—the mountains, canyons, lakes, and buttes—was created by past geologic events and processes. The vegetation growing in various wildlife habitats is a direct result of these geologic processes. This explains why trees grow in some areas and sagebrush in others, and why some mammals and birds are found where they are.

Geologists believe Earth to be 5 or 6 billion years old. The oldest rock outcroppings in Jackson Hole are the gneisses and schists of the Teton Range. These rocks solidified 2.5 to 3.5 billion years ago, in the Precambrian era, long before any plant or animal life existed. During millions of geologically dynamic years, many alterations occurred in these rocks that are visible today. An example is areas where molten streams of light-colored granite forced themselves into darker gneisses and schists. You may see this along canyon trails between Teton peaks. A dramatic example of a geologic alteration seen easily from turnouts along Teton Park Road is the enormous diabase dike that intruded Mount Moran 1.3 billion years ago. The black seam runs vertically, 100 to 150 feet wide, through Mount Moran and 7 miles to the west.

As the Earth cooled over the next few hundred million years, the forces of erosion leveled the Precambrian landscape (including the site of what was to become Jackson Hole) into a vast, featureless plain.

Early life began on Earth about 600 million years ago in the Paleozoic era. For the next half billion years, this great, flat plain was repeatedly subjected to flooding by shallow inland seas. The sediment deposited on Precambrian rock by these seas hardened into horizontal blankets. These layers of rock contain fossils of Paleozoic plant and animal life that help tell the geologic story. Sedimentary layers from different ages of the Paleozoic era can be seen in Jackson Hole today: gray dolomite from the Permian age, red and gray sandstone from the Pennsylvanian, blue-gray limestone from the Mississippian, and other layers of dolomite, limestone, and shale from earlier ages. Sloping layers of dolomite and limestone (deposited during a 200 million-year period beginning 500 million years ago) are visible on Teton peaks just south of Rendezvous Mountain.

Meanwhile, other geologic forces were affecting the Earth, including the area that would become known as Jackson Hole. The theory of plate tectonics helps explain the slow movement of continents over the face of the Earth. On the Atlantic Ocean floor, for millions of years, volcanic forces have been continuously creating new crust along the Mid-Atlantic ridge. As crust is added to the eastern edge of the North American plate, it moves westward away from the Mid-Atlantic ridge. The North American plate, being more buoyant than the Pacific plate, rides over and subducts it, or pushes it down. This subduction, occurring 90 million years ago as the North American plate was pushed over the Pacific plate, created much stress. This set the stage, about 80 million years ago, for one of the most dramatic scenes in North America's geologic play—the birth of the Rocky Mountains.

The collision between the North American and Pacific plates and the subduction of the latter resulted in compression on the western edge of the North American continent. One response to this compression was the formation of an ancient Teton Range, a broad arch or dome over present-day Jackson Hole from the Teton Range to the Gros Ventre Mountains. At that time, the area that was to become Jackson Hole was higher than the present-day Tetons and Gros Ventre Mountains.

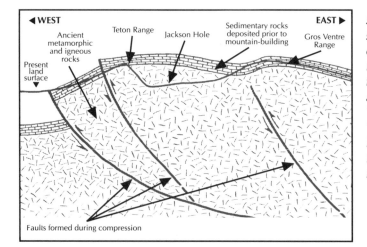

Simplified schematic cross-section illustrating the formation of an ancient Teton Range. The present land surface is shown for reference.

For millions of years the ancient Teton Range, or dome, continued to be subjected to geologic forces. Simultaneously, erosion was having a leveling effect. Then, about 50 million years ago, volcanoes began erupting in the Yellowstone and Absaroka region, distributing debris over immense areas. About 10 million years ago, a large freshwater lake submerged Jackson Hole and, for 5 million years, deposited a total of 5,000 feet of sediment known as the Teewinot Formation. Outcroppings of these strata of limestone, claystone, and tuff are exposed in the National Elk Refuge and on Blacktail Butte.

After millions of years of compression, about 9 to 11 million years ago, Jackson Hole began to be subjected to extension, or pulling apart. This created a different stress, faulting and tilting rather than folding, and the resulting earthquakes and faults began to wreak geologic havoc. One major fault system, the Teton Fault, is responsible for the creation of Jackson Hole and the Teton Range. Many other lesser faults left their marks on the landscape as well, some of the most noticeable being East and West Gros Ventre and Miller buttes, and the east-west fault scarp just south of the Gros Ventre River that leaves the town of Jackson 150 feet below the river bottom.

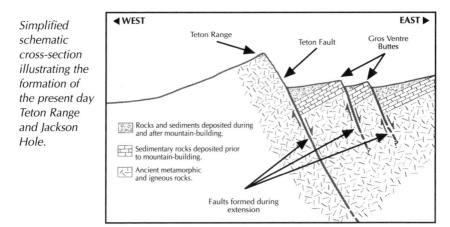

Simplified schematic cross-section illustrating the formation of the present day Teton Range and Jackson Hole.

Based on geologic evidence, then, the western edge of Jackson Hole—the line where the valley meets the base of the Teton Range—was, millions of years ago, higher than the Tetons. It also tells us that Jackson Hole continues to sink along the Teton Fault. As the valley sinks, it puts tremendous pressure on the molten layer far below. The sinking valley displaces the molten rock, which in turn pushes the Teton Range up, on the average, 1 inch for every 4 inches the valley floor drops.

Consider the following evidence supporting this geologic theory of how Jackson Hole was formed:

1. Flat tops on the highest peaks of the Gros Ventre, Wind River, and Absaroka ranges mark the remnants of the once vast plain that connected these ranges and dramatize the erosive effect of wind and water.

2. The western slopes of the Teton Range and the valley's buttes are gentle; their eastern slopes are precipitous. This profile is typical of faulting.

3. In addition to the steep eastern slope, other evidence of the Teton Fault includes lack of foothills, the asymmetry of the range, and visible fault scarps. An excellent example of a fault scarp lies at the base of Rockchuck Peak and can be seen by looking west from the Cathedral Group scenic pullout on the Jenny Lake Loop.

Fault Scarp at base of Rockchuck Peak

4. Sedimentary layers on the Gros Ventre Mountains are the same as those on the western slopes of the Tetons. Yet the Tetons, which have had all the sedimentary layers eroded away, still rise above these mountains to the east and west, indicating they have been uplifted at a rate exceeding the erosion.

5. Fish Creek flows along the western edge of the valley 15 feet lower than the Snake River, indicating the valley is still sinking along the Teton Fault plane. Only dikes built to contain the Snake prevent the river from working its way to the west and joining Fish Creek much farther north than is now the case.

The most recent chapter in the shaping of the Jackson Hole landscape was written by Ice Age glaciers. Glaciers form during periods when more snow falls during the winter than melts during the summer. The accumulating weight compresses the snow and changes it to ice. The ice mass increases over the years and begins to flow in response to gravitational forces. Like a giant, sloppy conveyor belt, the flowing ice carries rocks and debris downward and forward, often spilling them off to the side.

Often glaciers sculpt giant amphitheaters with steep walls (called cirques) at their head where they are at their maximum thickness and power. The head of Teton Glacier offers such an example. The floor of a cirque is frequently scooped so that a shallow basin remains. Amphitheater, Surprise, and Solitude lakes fill such ice-scooped basins.

Glaciers become efficient transporters of rocks, boulders, and other debris. This is especially true along the steep, eastern slopes of the Teton Range. The heavy powerful ice carves and scrapes the bottoms and walls of the canyon. Evidence today can be found in the polished and grooved rock surfaces on the floor of Glacier Gulch. Although canyons carved by streams usually are V-shaped, glaciers typically leave U-shaped canyons. Cascade Canyon is a good example of a U-shaped canyon.

The debris deposits of a glacier at its sides and ends are called lateral and terminal moraines, respectively. Part of the trail to Amphitheater Lake lies on a lateral moraine. Terminal moraines impound the lakes at the foot of the Tetons and, as tree-covered ridges, stretch across the valley floor.

When glaciers melt, vast quantities of water seek outlets. Streams filled with glacial flour and debris flow from the glacier's foot. As the glacier recedes, large gravel outwash plains are left. Much of the southern part of Jackson Hole is an outwash plain.

At least twice in the last 250,000 years, mighty rivers of ice poured out of the surrounding mountains into Jackson Hole, leaving their marks on the valley in major ways. The most extensive of these great ice movements took place about 150,000 years ago. Glaciers flowed south out of the Beartooth and Absaroka ranges (northeast and east of Jackson Hole) and were joined by another ice mass from the Wind River and Gros Ventre ranges (east and southeast of Jackson Hole). Up to 2,000 feet of ice blanketed the valley floor and completely covered Signal Mountain, Blacktail Butte, the Gros Ventre Buttes, and most of the Sleeping Indian. When these glaciers receded, the prodigious amounts of melting water washed away the soil that had accumulated on the valley floor and left behind a covering of quartzite boulders.

Another major ice movement, about half as extensive as the one above, began flowing into the valley between 70,000 and 80,000 years ago. Large lobes of ice came from the Absarokas down the Buffalo River Valley and the Pacific Creek drainage and later joined ice flowing from the Yellowstone Plateau and the Tetons. The moraines and outwash deposits of this glacier in the southern part of the valley were not reached by subsequent glaciers and are covered by windblown silt called loess. Badgers, coyotes, and other mammals use these loess-covered areas for dens and burrows.

A third ice movement, probably a phase of the previous glaciation, invaded the valley during a period that probably lasted from 25,000 to 10,000 years ago. Indians living in the area likely witnessed the glacier's later stages. This glaciation was of great importance because it left many prominent features of the present-day landscape. Ice flowed from the Tetons out onto the floor of Jackson Hole. A series of densely forested moraines stretching across the valley, known collectively as the Burned Ridge Moraine, mark the southernmost advance of this glaciation. The glaciers deposited clay and silt, which retain water, as well as chemical elements, providing a fertile environment for trees.

Streams spread south from the glacier as the moraine was being formed, leaving a flat, gravelly outwash deposit over much of the valley. This porous covering retains little water and is covered with sagebrush and other hardy, low-growth plants.

When the glacier receded, depressions filled with ice and covered with outwash gravel remained. The ice eventually melted and left water-filled kettles or "potholes." Several of these kettles lie south of Signal Mountain.

The glacier that flowed from Yellowstone, from Leigh Canyon, and from other canyons to the north created the terminal moraine that contains Jackson Lake. Smaller glaciers coming from canyons to the south deposited terminal moraines that impounded their melt waters. Today Phelps, Taggart, Bradley, and Jenny lakes lie like a string of pearls at the base of the Teton Range, jewels wrought by the mighty glaciers.

The terrain and habitat that resulted from these geologic processes and events provide a home for the rich variety of animal life thriving in Jackson Hole today. The next section describes major habitats of this area and the wildlife they support.

HABITATS

Hikers often ask where to find wildlife. An understanding of habitat is helpful in answering this question, since animals do have preferred habitats. They need to provide themselves and their young with food, water, cover, and living space, and they generally use habitats that meet their specialized needs.

Hikers familiar with various habitats of an area and the behavior of animals in that area will see more wildlife. In this section we'll describe the types of habitats found along the trails, and which animals you'll find in which areas.

RIPARIAN

Grand Teton National Park is drained by three major rivers. Two are tributaries of the third, the Snake River. The Snake River flows from its headwaters through Yellowstone National Park then south through Jackson Hole. The first major stream coming from the east, the Buffalo Fork, flows through Buffalo Valley then joins the Snake River near Moran Junction. The Gros Ventre River also flows from the east and joins the Snake River at the north end of West Gros Ventre Butte.

Cottonwoods, willows, and blue spruce are the predominant trees growing along the rivers and streams. Shrubs such as bearberry honeysuckle, silverberry, buffaloberry, thimbleberry, and chokecherry thrive in the moist soil. Common flowers include columbine, monkey flower, mountain hollyhock, and lupine.

Mammals come to the streams to drink and take advantage of the nearby abundant vegetation that offers food and cover. Moose browse in the willow thickets. River-dwelling beavers feed on willows and burrow into banks. River otters feed mostly on fish and use riverbank burrows or old beaver lodges. Coyotes, bison, and mule deer also come to rivers and streams for water and shelter.

The bottomlands of the rivers and their tributaries support many birds. Some spend all their time in these areas, while others come only to feed and drink. Pelicans, goldeneyes, and mergansers can be found swimming on the streams. Dippers search for insect larvae in fast-moving creeks. Great blue herons and spotted sandpipers may be found on or near sandy shores. Ospreys and bald eagles nest in the cottonwoods near the banks, and willows and other shrubs provide habitat for a variety of songbirds.

LAKES, PONDS, AND NEARBY MARSHES

While the deep cold lakes at the foot of the Tetons (Jenny, Bradley, Taggart, and Phelps lakes) seldom attract much wildlife, Jackson Lake and other more shallow lakes and ponds with marshy surroundings support many animal populations in Grand Teton National Park.

The impounding of Jackson Lake has created thousands of acres of shallow water and, at low water, marshy and mud-flat habitat. A large percentage of the park's bird species may be found on or near Jackson Lake. Many ducks and other water birds feed on this large lake. The seasonal mud-flats to the north of the dam host many migratory shorebirds. The willowy, marshy areas near the lake's tributaries and the mixed woodlands and open brushy areas near the lake shores support a rich variety of birds.

Moose browse year-round in willow thickets found in the marshy areas near lakes and ponds. In summer they also wade into the ponds to feed on succulent aquatic vegetation. Beaver dam up streams to form ponds and build lodges of branches and saplings held together with mud. These nocturnal animals feed on willows, aspens, alders, and cottonwoods and are best seen early in the morning or late in the evening. Muskrats also use the lakes and ponds for their homes, and mule deer frequently can be seen drinking at water's edge.

Various willows, blue camas, bog orchids, cow-parsnip, and monkshood are plants that may be found near these lakes and ponds.

SAGEFLATS AND GRASSLANDS

Sagebrush grows on dry, porous soils. Much of the valley floor is covered with sagebrush. More than 100 species of native grasses and wildflowers also grow in this dry soil. Bitterbrush, sticky geranium, groundsel, pussytoes, larkspur, buckwheat, stonecrop, balsamroot, Indian paintbrush, harebells, and gilia are just some of the many plants found in this habitat.

Lack of cover makes large animals conspicuous. Pronghorns feed on sagebrush and grass and live exclusively in this habitat. Bison eat grasses and sedges and often graze in meadows and sagebrush flats. Coyotes come to sagebrush flats to prey on rodents. Elk use these meadows at night to graze on grasses and often will be found at dusk or dawn near the forest edges. Uinta ground squirrels, relatives of the prairie dog, live in burrows on the sageflats. They feed on plants and scavenge on carrion. Badgers also make their homes in burrows on the sageflats.

Vesper and Brewer's sparrows, sage thrashers, green-tailed towhees, and sage grouse can all be found in the sageflats. Long-billed curlews, western meadowlarks, mountain bluebirds, and savannah sparrows inhabit the grasslands.

FORESTED FOOTHILLS AND MORAINES

The eastern slope of the Teton Range was formed largely as the result of the valley floor slipping down the plane of the Teton Fault. Typically, mountains formed in this manner do not have foothills, and the Tetons are no exception. However, glaciers deposited debris along the base of the mountain range on which forests of lodgepole pine, Engelmann spruce, subalpine fir, and Douglas fir have grown. Aspens grow on moist morainal drainages.

Mountains on the east side of the valley tend to have foothills. Douglas fir forests generally grow on the north- and east-facing slopes.

South-facing hills are less heavily forested, with stands of lodgepole pine, quaking aspen, and a few very large Douglas firs interspersed with open areas.

Huckleberry, elderberry, and strawberry thrive in the shady, moist environment. Columbine, heartleaf arnica, phlox, pearly everlasting, and calypso orchid can also be found here.

Owls, goshawks, woodpeckers, flycatchers, and other songbirds inhabit the deep forests and are attracted to the open woods, aspen stands, and woodland margins as well. Hummingbirds, sparrows, and warblers like brushy, open meadows at forest edges.

Black bears frequent meadows and the lower parts of canyons, but are seldom far from the protective cover of trees. They feed on roots, berries, insects, small rodents, and carrion. Martens, arboreal members of the weasel family, inhabit older coniferous forests. They prey on squirrels, mice, and birds and scavenge on carrion. Red squirrels and snowshoe hares also inhabit forested foothills and moraines.

MOUNTAIN SLOPES AND CANYONS

Conifer forests comprised of lodgepole pine, Engelmann spruce, Douglas fir, and subalpine fir grow among rock outcroppings between the valley and the treeless alpine regions. Stands of whitebark pine occur above 8,000 feet; mountain meadows cover more of the mountainsides than forests do. Aspen stands become fewer and smaller than at lower elevations. Ravens, eagles, and jays frequent this habitat.

Some elk remain in the valley in the summer, but many migrate to the high country to feed. They prefer ecotones (edges) between forests and meadows. Mule deer migrate to the high country to browse on woody plants. They frequent open forests and meadow edges at dusk and dawn.

A great variety of plants thrive on the high mountainsides. Fireweed, cinquefoil, balsamroot, groundsel, lupine, and larkspur occupy the sunny mountain slopes. Ceanothus takes over in burned areas. Utah honeysuckle, huckleberry, gooseberry, serviceberry, and mountain ash form the understory in forested canyons.

ALPINE

At and above tree line, this high mountain habitat endures harsh weather conditions. Strong winds and low temperatures above 10,000 feet allow only low-growing vegetation. The growing season lasts only a few weeks; alpine plants begin flowering soon after the snow melts. Some species grow only in the alpine area; others grow tall at lower elevations but are dwarfed in their alpine version. Look for marsh marigold, hymenoxys, glacier lily, Parry primrose, mountainheather, moss campion, Indian paintbrush, sky pilot, and alpine forget-me-not. Vertical migrants, such as rosy finches and water pipits, nest here. Ravens, Clark's nutcrackers, and golden eagles all spend some time in this habitat.

Yellow-bellied marmots feed on vegetation and can be found in rocky places from moraines to above tree line. Pikas inhabit high canyons, and bighorn sheep graze the high country in summer, with a few inhabiting either end of the Tetons.

Black bear climbing tree.

BEARS

Few animals symbolize wilderness as impressively as bears. Grand Teton National Park is bear country. Grizzlies are seen with some frequency, mostly in the northern part of the park, although they may occur throughout. Black bears may be encountered almost anywhere in the park.

Bears are highly individualistic animals. Each responds to a situation based on its own life experiences. Traits common to all bears include a vigorous defense of a kill or food cache; typical of females is vehement protection of their cubs. Bears may charge or attack when they are startled at close range.

Learn to hike and camp safely in bear country—for your own protection and for the preservation of wild bears. Follow the precautions below to lessen the likelihood of an unpleasant encounter with a bear. Finally, be sure to report all bear sightings to a visitor center or ranger station.

WHERE AND WHEN YOU MIGHT SEE A BEAR: ANYTIME—ANYWHERE!

Bears are active day and night and have been observed in campgrounds, on canyon trails, around rivers and lakes, crossing roads, in sagebrush flats, and in developed areas. They are most common along the lower elevations of the Teton Range where lush vegetation occurs.

A FED BEAR IS A DEAD BEAR

Allowing a bear to obtain human food even once often results in aggressive behavior. Aggressive bears present a threat to human safety and eventually must be destroyed or removed from the park. Please obey the law and do not allow bears or other wildlife to obtain food meant for humans.

HOW TO PREVENT BEAR ENCOUNTERS WHILE HIKING

- Learn to identify black and grizzly bears—refer to their descriptions in the section, **Mammals**, page 133.

- Become familiar with bear signs (tracks, scat, diggings, ripped trees and logs) so that you can detect their presence before a bear sees you or you see it—refer to the section on **Reading the Landscape**, page 31.

- Usually bears will leave if they sense humans in the area. If a bear is upwind or near running water, it will not easily hear an intruder. To avoid surprising it, make <u>very loud</u> noises (shout, sing, or clap your hands) when hiking through dense vegetation or when coming to a blind bend in the trail.

- Avoid hiking alone or at night. Bears feed at all hours of the day and night.

- While hiking, look ahead for bears or their signs to avoid surprising them. Leave the area immediately if you see a bear. Never approach a bear, not even to obtain photographs.

- Leave an area where there is a dead animal—bears defend their kills and any carrion they are scavenging.

- Be very careful in areas where there are ripe berries, as this is a favorite food of bears.

- Do not leave packs containing food unattended, even for a few minutes.

WHEN CAMPING IN BEAR COUNTRY

- Hang food and anything odorous (soap, toothpaste, garbage) at least 10 to 12 feet off the ground, 4 to 6 feet from the tree trunk, and 4 to 6 feet below any large branches.

- Do not store anything odorous in a sleeping bag or tent. Use unscented soaps, deodorants, and cosmetics. Do not use perfumes.

- Keep food storage and cooking sites at least 100 yards from any sleeping areas. Use bearproof storage boxes where provided. Avoid cooking greasy or odorous foods. Do not sleep in the same clothes that you wore while cooking.

- Keep a clean camp. Pack out all garbage; do not bury it. Do not cook or eat in a tent.

- Leave empty packs with zippers open, outside and away from the tent.

IF YOU ENCOUNTER A BEAR

- Keep calm. Do not run. It is impossible to outrun bears, as they can run over 30 miles per hour. Besides, running often elicits attacks from otherwise nonaggressive bears.

- If the bear is unaware of you, turn around and return the way you came or detour quietly yet quickly away from the bear, giving it as wide a berth as possible.

- If the bear is aware of you and is nearby but has not acted aggressively, slowly back away, talking in an even tone while slowly waving your arms. If possible, move upwind so the bear can smell you. Once it has identified you as a human, it may leave.

- Climbing a tree is not recommended. Even if a tree is present, it may be very difficult to climb—and the chances are that, if you can climb it, so can the bear.

- Grizzlies are thought to be more aggressive than black bears. All female bears with cubs tend to be aggressive. A bear may appear to be alone, but may actually be a female with cubs that are not visible.

IF A BEAR APPROACHES OR CHARGES

- Do not run; this probably increases the chance of an attack.

- Drop something to distract the bear—preferably nothing that contains food, but a jacket, camera, binoculars, or this book.

- Do not drop a pack; it helps protect the body in case of an attack.

- Bluff charges are often used to scare people away, with the bear stopping before contact. Bear experts generally recommend standing still until the bear stops, then talking softly, averting your gaze, and backing off slowly.

- If the bear continues the charge and is about to hit you or does hit you, drop to the ground and play dead. Lie on your stomach, lock fingers behind your neck so your arms and elbows will protect your head and face, draw knees up to your chest, and don't move. This is the best position to protect vital organs. A pack will help protect your back. Try not to move or scream if clawed or bitten. Your best hope is that the bear will think you are dead and will no longer feel threatened. If it starts to leave, listen carefully and do not move until you are sure it has left the area.

IF A BEAR ENTERS THE CAMPING AREA

- If a bear enters the campsite while you are there but not in the tent, follow the guidelines above.

- If you are in a tent and hear a bear in the campsite, turn on a flashlight inside the tent and talk in a calm manner to let the bear know there are humans present.

- If a bear drags a sleeping person from a tent, he or she should fight back, and the other people in the campsite should do anything possible to distract the bear. This is an especially dangerous situation, because the bear has grabbed someone who certainly was not a threat. The person being dragged away will almost certainly be killed if the bear is not distracted.

NOTE: Spray canisters containing an extract of cayenne pepper are now available at camping and outdoor stores. This product seems to be very effective as a bear repellent, but only at very close range. If you decide to carry this product, you should consider these points:

- Keep the product immediately available at all times. It will do no good if it's packed away when you need it. Some of the products come in a holster.

- The spray must hit the bear in the eyes and nose. The effective range when there is no wind is only about 20 feet. A good strategy might be to start spraying before the bear comes that close so that a "wall" of spray is created.

- Practice a few times with the canister to become familiar with its operation before taking it to the backcountry.

- If there is a crosswind or, worse yet, a headwind, the spray will be rendered largely ineffective on the bear and might even blow into your eyes.

- At best, this product will be effective only in highly specific circumstances. At worst, it can give you a false sense of security and even backfire if not used properly or if there is wind. Follow the above precautions and try to avoid situations where this product would be needed.

All of this information about the danger posed by bears is not meant to frighten anyone away from hiking and camping in the park. Considering the thousands of people who hike here, there are very few cases of unpleasant bear experiences. The odds are slight that you will have such an encounter with a bear, especially if you follow the guidelines we've provided. Nevertheless, it is normal to feel a concern about bears in the wilderness. It is up to each individual to decide whether this concern will ruin an otherwise enjoyable experience in the backcountry.

Beavers inhabit ponds or dam streams
to create their required habitat.

READING THE LANDSCAPE

The landscape may be read like a book. Your interest and level of awareness dictate what fills the pages. Picture a mountain canyon surrounded by jagged peaks. A glacial geologist knows that glaciers have sculpted the canyon because of its U-shaped profile. A mountain climber sees routes to the top of peaks towering above the canyon. An angler viewing the same canyon turns to the creek draining it where fish lurk in deep pools. Birds singing in the willows along the creek attract the attention of a birder. Trackers search for recent history: tracks, droppings, and other signs of animals frequenting the canyon. A wildflower enthusiast notes meadows that are carpeted with colorful blossoms.

Geologic history explains the big picture of why the natural landscape looks the way it does. Geology also accounts for the types of soils found. Soils, moisture, aspect, climate, and other factors determine which plants grow in an area. Plant-eating animals inhabit places where their food grows, and predators follow their prey. Animals and plants interact with each other and their environment, leaving telltale indications behind.

Alert observers may detect everything from landscape-shaping geological processes to the kinds of animals present by paying attention to their surroundings. Reading the landscape is as challenging as solving a mystery—clues abound. The advantage of reading the landscape is an exhilarating sense of belonging, of becoming an insider outside.

Finding mammal tracks, scats, and other signs provides hikers with valuable information: who shares their trail. Where bears, moose, and other large animals are found, reading the landscape for animal activity is a necessity. This section on reading mammal signs has been included to add to your hiking comfort and safety.

TRACKS

Identifying tracks is not always easy. Try to find one very clear track. Other possible signs in the area combined with what is known about the animal's behavior will also be helpful in identifying the animal.

Tracks With Two Toes

In mud and snow, sometimes ungulate tracks will reveal two smaller toe prints in addition to the two larger ones. These are made by the dewclaws, two small toes farther up the back of the animal's foot.

DEER—Deer tracks range in length from 1.5 inches (fawns) to 3 inches (large bucks). Deer frequent open forests and meadow edges. Often tracks of the deer's hind feet overlap those of its front feet. The distance between tracks when the deer is striding is usually about 20 inches.

MOOSE—Moose tracks range in length from 2.5 inches (young calf) to 7 inches (large bull). A calf with tracks less than 3 inches would still be with its mother, and probably her tracks will also be there. By the time a calf leaves its mother, its track will be longer than the largest deer. The distance between tracks may be as much as 5 feet.

ELK—Elk tracks average 4.5 inches in length; generally they are larger than deer tracks and smaller than moose tracks. The distance between an elk's tracks is usually at least 2 feet but not over 3 feet.

PRONGHORN—Pronghorn (antelope) tracks average about the same size as deer tracks. But pronghorn habitat, dry sagebrush flats, is not appealing to deer. The distance between tracks ordinarily ranges from 12 to 20 inches.

BIGHORN SHEEP—The tracks of this animal are also similar to those of deer and average about 3 inches in length. But their summer habitat, high mountain slopes, is not where deer are likely to be found. The distance between tracks is about 15 inches.

BISON—Bison tracks are almost as wide (5 inches) as they are long (6 inches). Like deer, the rear tracks sometimes overlap the front tracks. There are usually less than 3 feet between the tracks.

TRACKS WITH FOUR TOES

COYOTE—The track of a coyote has four toe prints, usually with claws, and a triangular heel pad. The track averages 2.5 inches in adults. The tracks of wolves (which are extremely rare in the park) are twice as large. It is easy to confuse coyote tracks with dog tracks of similar size, but dogs are not permitted on trails or in the backcountry, and their tracks should not be found.

SNOWSHOE HARE—These tracks show four toe prints, sometimes with claws. The round front tracks are about 1.75 inches long. The rear tracks are very large (5 to 6 inches long) and account for the snowshoe name.

TRACKS WITH FIVE TOES

BLACK BEAR—
Occasionally the little toe does not show in the track, making it appear to be four-toed. The track has claws and a heel pad. The rear track is very large (6 to 9 inches long and 3 to 4 inches wide) and has a long heel pad. The front track is about 4 inches long and has a much smaller heel pad. The claws extend .5 inch in front of the toe pads (about 1 inch for grizzlies).

 **GRIZZLY BEAR**—The tracks of a grizzly are very similar to those of a black bear. The grizzly's toes are closer together and less arched. While the little toe of the black bear is not as far forward as the big toe, the grizzly's little toe is just about directly across from the big toe. The claws of the grizzly extend about 1 inch in front of the toe pads. The claws of the black bear extend about .5 inch.

SCATS

The droppings of a species, called scats by wildlife biologists, vary greatly depending upon the time of year and the size and diet of the animal. For this reason, scats should be treated as one clue among other signs in trying to identify an animal's presence. On the other hand, some scats are fairly distinctive in color and shape and do provide reliable identification.

The scats described below are those of larger mammals commonly found on or near the park's trails.

In the spring and early summer, the scats of deer, elk, and moose often cannot be distinguished from one another. The water content of food is much higher at this time, and scats become amorphous and sometimes look like cowpies. When bears are feeding on berries, their scats also may be amorphous but can be distinguished from moose scats by the preponderance of berry seeds.

DEER—Usually deer droppings are easy to identify. Dark, cylindrical pellets are .75 to 1 inch long and about 3/8 inch in diameter. Pellets have one flat or concave end and one pointed end.

 **MOOSE**—Pellets are larger than those of deer (about 1 to 1.5 inches long and .75 inch in diameter) and usually not as dark in color. Their shape is round on both ends.

 **ELK**—The size of elk pellets is about midway between deer and moose. Their shape is similar to that of deer pellets—pointed on one end and flat or concave on the other.

COYOTE—Like humans, coyotes like to use trails, and their scats are frequently seen on or along trails. Scats are 2-5 inches long and .75 inch or more in diameter. Usually one or both ends are pointed, and they often contain hair (from the coyote's prey).

BEAR—Grizzly scats are virtually indistinguishable from those of black bears. They are usually broken into segments 2 to 3 inches long and 1.25 to 1.5 inches in diameter. They are cylindrical and have flat ends. Scats contain items reflecting the current diet of the bear: insects, hair, and bits of vegetation. During berry season, scats can be amorphous and even look like cowpies.

OTHER SIGNS

Humans have changed their environment more than any other animal. But other animals also change their surroundings and leave signs indicating where they have done so. Some of these signs are very obvious such as nests, dens, and dams. Others are more subtle: injuries to trees, digging, tunneling, trails, runways, beds, natural cavities, food remains, and caches.

Some commonly seen signs are included below. Finding these signs and understanding their purpose as well as identifying the animal that caused them can be very rewarding. Reading signs that help to determine when bears are present can help you avoid encountering them.

BARK SCRAPED, RUBBED, OR PEELED

Several mammals remove large areas of bark from trees: elk, deer, moose, porcupines, and bears. The most common type of bark removal is caused by male deer, elk, and moose rubbing their antlers against trees to remove the velvety covering. Rubs often begin a few inches off the ground and extend as high as the antlered animal can reach. Young trees and saplings are preferred. Trees are rubbed after antler growth is complete during late summer or early fall.

Porcupines remove large areas of bark by chewing. The animal usually sits on a high limb next to the trunk and eats the outer bark from an area as far as it can reach.

Bears remove bark from a tree in two ways, for different reasons. One method occurs commonly in winter. When the animal leaves its winter den, it is hungry. Often snow cover is still heavy, and the food supply is limited. The bear will tear bark off conifer trees with its teeth, sometimes girdling the tree, starting at its base and continuing as high as the bear can reach. It then chews at the cambium, leaving teeth marks on the inner wood. Strips of the outer bark remain hanging from the trunk.

Another type of bark removal caused by bears typically takes place in the summer and serves the social purpose of creating a mark. This occurs on large trees and is usually high off the ground. The bear stands on its hind legs and scrapes the bark with its claws. The bear will do this repeatedly, sometimes whenever it passes the spot. It will also rub its back against the tree, often leaving hairs stuck to the tree. Bears have five claws on each foot, and groups of five parallel claw marks may be seen on the tree.

Sometimes an additional bear sign may be seen: claw marks on smooth-barked trees, like aspens, made when bears climb the trees.

LOGS RIPPED APART

Logs rotting on the ground host large populations of insects. With powerful swipes of their forepaws, bears tear the logs apart to feed on anything living in the wood, especially ants and grubs.

PART II
TRAIL DESCRIPTIONS

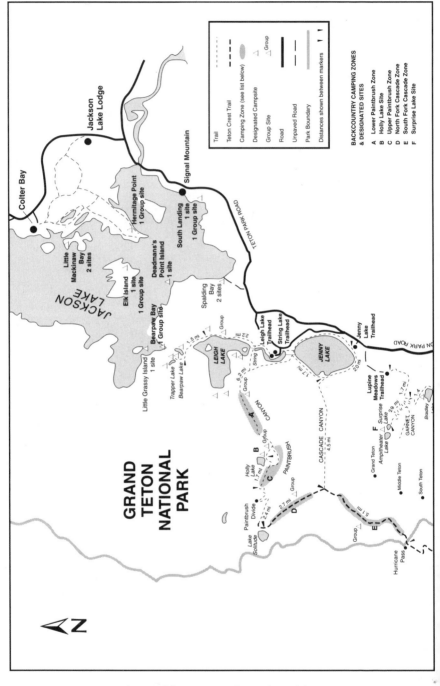

LUPINE MEADOWS TO LEIGH LAKE MAP

SOUTH TETON TRAILS FROM LUPINE MEADOWS TO LEIGH LAKE

LUPINE MEADOWS TO AMPHITHEATER LAKE AND GARNET CANYON
JENNY LAKE LOOP AND MOOSE PONDS TRAIL
STRING LAKE TO BEARPAW LAKE AND TRAPPER LAKE (via Leigh Lake)
CASCADE CANYON
    SOUTH FORK OF CASCADE CANYON TO HURRICANE PASS
    CASCADE CANYON TO LAKE SOLITUDE
    LAKE SOLITUDE TO PAINTBRUSH DIVIDE
PAINTBRUSH CANYON TO PAINTBRUSH DIVIDE

LUPINE MEADOWS TO AMPHITHEATER LAKE
AND GARNET CANYON

This hike is almost 10 miles round trip. However, it is one of the shortest trails into the mountains. It is also the approach to numerous technical and nontechnical climbs of Teton peaks, and it involves lots of uphill walking.

The trail presents extraordinary views of the valley as it ascends forested moraines and switchbacks across flower-filled slopes. It climbs through the subalpine zone to the very base of an enormous glacial cirque at the head of the Burned Wagon Gulch drainage. This is one of the best hikes to observe how gains in elevation affect the development of flowers. For example, in late spring when balsamroot has finished blooming in the valley, it will be in full, glorious bloom in higher mountain meadows.

Usually snow remains on the upper trail from mid- to late June. An early start is recommended in order to avoid midday heat when walking up the steep open switchbacks.

LENGTH: 9.6 miles. The trail to Amphitheater Lake is 4.8 miles each way. A spur trail to Garnet Canyon splits off the Amphitheater Lake Trail at 3 miles and continues another 1.1 miles, for a round-trip of 8.2 miles. The round-trip hike to Amphitheater Lake and Garnet Canyon is 11.8 miles. The hike to Garnet Canyon is described after the following Amphitheater Lake description.

At a well-marked junction (1.7 miles), a branch of the trail leads to Bradley Lake and is described in the **Valley Trail** section.

DIFFICULTY: The hike to Amphitheater Lake is rated *difficult* and requires that the hiker be fit and acclimated to the Jackson Hole altitude. There is no technical climbing, but the trail does gain elevation steadily for more than 4.5 miles. The trail is well marked.

ELEVATION: The hike begins at 6,762 feet (in the parking area) and climbs to 9,698 feet at Amphitheater Lake, a gain of almost 3,000 feet. The Garnet Canyon spur climbs to 8,900 feet, a gain of over 2,100 feet.

ACCESS: From the Moose Entrance Station in Grand Teton National Park, drive north on Teton Park Road for 6.6 miles. Turn left at Lupine Meadows Junction and follow the signs to Lupine Meadows Trailhead (about 2 miles).

MAP: Lupine Meadows to Leigh Lake, page 38.

TRAIL DESCRIPTION: As you begin your hike at Lupine Meadows Trailhead, you will notice that this area lives up to its name. In the late spring and summer, colorful lupines blanket any surface not occupied by sagebrush.

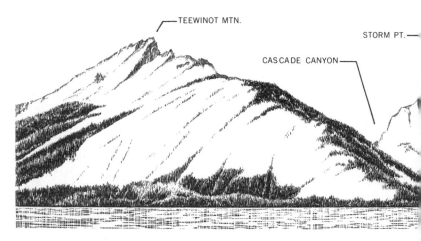

TEEWINOT MTN.

STORM PT.

CASCADE CANYON

The contrast in plant life that is evident near the parking area was caused by two different glacial phenomena. The sagebrush flats are part of the outwash plain deposited by glacial meltwaters. The area consists of gravel and cobblestones which retain little moisture and support only hardy, drought-tolerant plants like sagebrush and lupine.

Next to the parking area grows a different plant community—a mixed conifer forest thriving on thick, morainal soil that holds the moisture required by these trees. Moisture-demanding flowering plants such as green gentian grow among the rocks scattered in the rich soil.

These two different plant communities in turn support different animals. A walk through the sagebrush is likely to produce sightings of vesper and Brewer's sparrows and, possibly, pronghorns. The wet bottomland forest of lodgepole and subalpine fir near the trailhead attracts woodpeckers, thrushes, kinglets, and mule deer.

The trail cuts through the moist conifer forest for a few hundred yards before gaining elevation. Ospreys have nested in the trees where the trail begins to climb.

Large gneiss boulders can be seen along the trail. Did movement along the Teton Fault cause them to roll down onto the moraine? Were they carried here by the "conveyor belt" action of glaciers? They could have arrived by either process.

As the trail climbs the moraine, it tracks the northeast slope and enters a Douglas fir stand where Williamson's sapsuckers have nested. The more open areas of this section of trail support an abundance of plants preferring moist soil. Shrubs such as honeysuckle, serviceberry, gooseberry, huckleberry, and mountain ash may be found along this stretch. Leopard lilies and calypso orchids are among the many flowers lining the path.

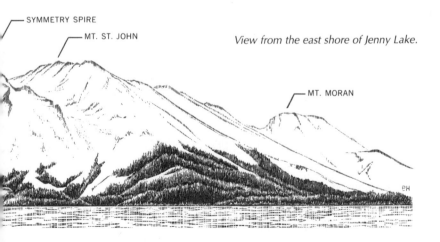

SYMMETRY SPIRE

MT. ST. JOHN

View from the east shore of Jenny Lake.

MT. MORAN

PH

The trail follows the crest of a forested ridge with Glacier Gulch to the north and Burned Wagon Gulch to the south, and parallel ridges beyond both ravines. These ridges are lateral glacial moraines.

At 1.7 miles, the Amphitheater Lake Trail intersects the Valley Trail. From this point the hike continues straight and up. The branch to the left is described in the **Valley Trail** section.

Soon the trail begins to gain altitude rapidly through a series of switchbacks. Traverses cut through flower-filled meadows and over numerous seeps. Many of the seeps are results of faulting that created weak spots for the water to "seep" out of the mountainside.

Balsamroots flourish on the sunny slopes. Bog orchids, monkey flowers, and other water-loving plants can be found by seeps. Snowbrush ceanothus also prospers on the sunny mountain slopes. This plant often establishes itself quickly in burned areas.

The traverses of the switchbacks afford excellent views of Bradley Lake which lies just below. Taggart Lake and the surrounding burn area lie to the south of Bradley Lake (see section on **Taggart Lake Loop** for a description of the fire).

At 3 miles the trail forks. The fork to the left goes 1.1 miles to Garnet Canyon. This trail provides access to many Teton climbs and is described after the Amphitheater Lake description.

The trail has now arrived at 8,000 feet in elevation, and white-bark pine is becoming more prevalent. From this height the ridge separating Taggart and Bradley lakes is visible. This ridge is a common lateral moraine for the two mountain glaciers that flowed down Avalanche Canyon and Garnet Canyon. The terminal moraines of these glaciers impounded the two lakes.

After leaving the Garnet Canyon intersection, the trail heads north. Above the lower open slopes, subalpine firs dominate the forest. As the trail climbs higher, whitebark pine becomes the dominant species. Both bears and Clark's nutcrackers are fond of whitebark pine nuts, and nutcrackers are almost solely responsible for the distribution of this tree's seeds.

Many of the plants found in alpine areas are also found in this subalpine zone. The birds found here—Clark's nutcrackers, pine gros-beaks, rosy finches—are vertical migrants: they winter in the valley and summer at high elevations.

Even on a warm day, the air begins to get noticeably cooler as the trail approaches tree line and enters the mountains, leaving the valley views behind. The cirque walls at the head of this ancient glacial drainage dwarf everything. Disappointment Peak guards the natural amphitheater, and Teepe Pillar, Teewinot Mountain, Mount Owen, and the Grand Teton all stand in reserve.

It's just a few steps farther to Surprise Lake, a perfect circle of a tarn in a perfect subalpine setting. Like Amphitheater Lake a few hundred yards beyond, this lake resulted from meltwater filling a basin scooped out of the floor of the cirque by a massive glacier. The pinnacle southeast of the outlet from Surprise Lake offers exceptional views.

Continue on the short distance to Amphitheater Lake which lies at 9,698 feet, very close to tree line (1.6 miles from the Garnet Canyon Fork and 4.6 miles from the parking area). A few stunted and twisted trees grow on the slopes above the lake. Strong winds, a short growing season, and punishing snow and ice make it too tough for all but the smallest and hardiest of plants.

From Amphitheater Lake, the trail leads a little farther up to a saddle overlooking Glacier Gulch. To return to the parking area, simply retrace your steps.

GARNET CANYON TRAIL

The Garnet Canyon Trail follows the slope contour around and up into Garnet Canyon, providing magnificent views of the heart of the Tetons from the canyon entrance. The trail ends at a massive boulder field below the Platforms, a designated camping area for climbers.

Continuing beyond the end of the trail requires mountaineering skills including route-finding, bouldering, and snow and ice techniques. Climbers and mountaineers are encouraged to register at the Jenny Lake Ranger Station (mid-May to late September) or the Moose Visitor Center permits desk (late September to mid-May) to obtain information on routes and current conditions. Camping in Garnet Canyon requires a free permit.

Middle Teton from the end of Garnet Canyon Trail. The conspicuous vertical black column is an intruded diabase dike.

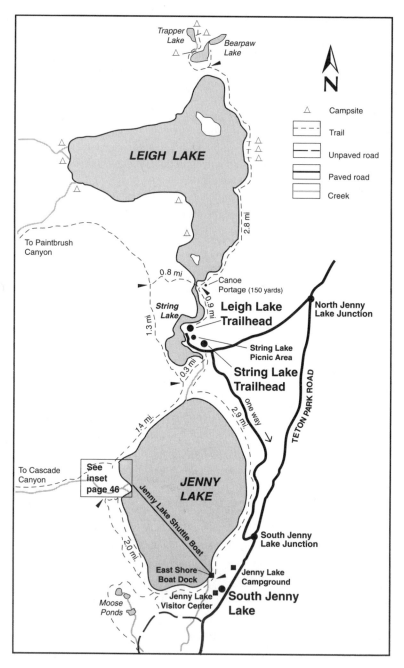

Trapper Lake

Bearpaw Lake

N

△ Campsite

--- Trail

Unpaved road

Paved road

Creek

LEIGH LAKE

T
T

2.8 mi

To Paintbrush Canyon

0.8 mi

Canoe Portage (150 yards)

0.9 mi

String Lake

Leigh Lake Trailhead

North Jenny Lake Junction

1.3 mi

String Lake Picnic Area

String Lake Trailhead

0.3 mi

2.9 mi

one way

TETON PARK ROAD

1.4 mi.

To Cascade Canyon

See inset page 46

JENNY LAKE

Jenny Lake Shuttle Boat

2.0 mi.

South Jenny Lake Junction

East Shore Boat Dock

Jenny Lake Campground

Moose Ponds

Jenny Lake Visitor Center

South Jenny Lake

LEIGH LAKE AND JENNY LAKE MAP

JENNY LAKE LOOP

The trails around Jenny Lake offer some of the most impressive scenery in Grand Teton National Park. They are also some of the most popular. The magnificent setting combined with relatively easy access to spectacular mountain trails make this area the first choice of many hikers.

Jenny Lake was named after the Shoshone wife of mountain man, Beaver Dick Leigh. Beaver Dick was one of Jackson Hole's early settlers. The lake is 2.5 miles long and 1.5 miles wide. Like the floor of the valley itself, Jenny Lake slopes to the west, making the west side of the lake deepest. This accounts for the lake's elongated shape. The glacier flowing out of Cascade Canyon thousands of years ago spread to the north and south rather than flowing up the valley's grade to the east. When the glacier receded, it left a terminal moraine much wider than the mouth of the canyon. Today conifer forests encircle the lake and thrive on the hospitable soil of glacial deposits.

LENGTH: The distance around the lake is 7 miles. However, the hike can be abbreviated by taking the boat shuttle crossing the lake in either direction. The ride across the lake takes only a few minutes and offers fine views of the mountains. The shuttle operates in the summer months; call (307) 733-2703 for the current schedule and rates.

DIFFICULTY: The hike around Jenny Lake is rated *easy.* The relatively flat trail rarely rises more than a few feet above the lake. The trail is wide, well marked, and well maintained, and the footing is good.

ELEVATION: Jenny Lake lies at 6,783 feet. The trail varies little from 6,800 feet.

ACCESS: To String Lake parking area, drive 11 miles north on Teton Park Road from Moose Entrance Station to North Jenny Lake Junction, then turn left and follow the signs. The trailhead is just south of the parking area.

To Jenny Lake parking area, drive 6.8 miles from Moose Entrance Station to South Jenny Lake Junction. Turn left into the parking area and follow signs to the East Shore Boat Dock.

NOTE: In summer, these parking areas frequently are full during the middle part of the day.

MAP: Leigh Lake and Jenny Lake, page 44.

TRAIL DESCRIPTION: The hike around Jenny Lake can originate from either parking area. The route described below begins at String Lake parking area and follows the west shore around the south end then returns via the east shore of Jenny Lake.

The String Lake Trailhead lies to the south of the parking area. If hiking in the spring, you may be fortunate enough to spot harlequin ducks on String Lake. A footbridge crosses the outlet from String Lake to Jenny Lake, and signs point the way to Hidden Falls. The trail then follows the outlet creek on its west side through a conifer forest. Rapids near the head of Jenny Lake indicate that it is about 40 feet lower than String Lake. The trail follows the northwest shore of Jenny Lake as the forest becomes Douglas and subalpine fir. Several small drainages create moist, open areas with multitudes of flowers.

Just before reaching the West Shore Boat Dock, the trail crosses a creek flowing out of Hanging Canyon. The boat dock is 2.1 miles from the parking area.

Several options are offered at the West Shore Boat Dock. You can take a launch across the lake (a fee is charged) which cuts 2 miles from the hike around the lake. Or you can follow the trail to Hidden Falls, Inspiration Point, and on to Cascade Canyon (see **Cascade Canyon**). Or, the trail continues around the lake, as you can follow in the description below.

The trail from the West Shore Boat Dock around the south side of the lake leads through a

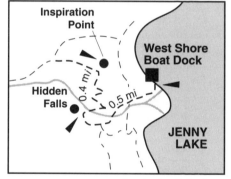

Inspiration Point inset.

spruce/fir forest next to the lake. The understory of serviceberry soon gives way to thimbleberry and columbine growing in profusion among large, glacially deposited boulders. Bog orchids thrive in the shady, moist soil near the seeps and the springs trickling from the forest floor. Thrushes sing from the understory, and tanagers sing from the canopy.

As the trail nears the south end of the lake, an overlook provides a good view of the three small lakes called Moose Ponds. A few hundred yards farther lies an intersection with a trail looping around Moose Ponds. This diversion is described next; the Jenny Lake Loop description continues after the following guide to Moose Ponds Trail.

MOOSE PONDS TRAIL

Moose Ponds are located at the base of Teewinot Mountain and afford a superb view of the jagged spires crowning the peak. The ponds and adjacent marshes provide habitat for waterfowl and other birds, while the lower slopes of Teewinot Mountain support an array of large animals including elk, moose, mule deer, and black bears. Red squirrels chatter from the conifer forests on the south side of the ponds, and yellow-bellied marmots sun themselves on boulders in open meadows. The large boulders scattered along the base of the mountains may have been transported by glaciers, or their presence may attest to old earthquake activity along the Teton Fault that hurtled the rocks down to the valley.

LENGTH: This loop adds 2 miles to the Jenny Lake Loop.

DIFFICULTY: Because this trail is at valley level, relatively flat and short, this hike is rated as *easy*.

ELEVATION: Moose Ponds are at about 6,800 feet.

ACCESS: Parking is available at South Jenny Lake parking area. The trail along the southern edge of Jenny Lake leads west to Moose Ponds Trail.

MAP: Leigh Lake and Jenny Lake, page 44.

TRAIL DESCRIPTION: From the junction with Jenny Lake Trail, Moose Ponds Trail first skirts the lower edge of the moraine separating the ponds and Jenny Lake. The trail then crosses a willow marsh and leads gently uphill through a stand of young aspens and meadows of wildflowers. On the south side of the ponds, the trail passes through a forest of mature Engelmann spruce and subalpine fir. A footbridge spans a creek flowing from Teewinot Mountain on the west side of the trail.

After crossing a small patch of sagebrush meadow, the trail arrives at the south side of the third Moose Pond. The trail swings north and takes a direct line across the extensive sagebrush flats of Lupine Meadows, crossing the trailhead road twice. Hikers may choose to follow the unpaved trailhead road to the spur trail that connects with Jenny Lake Trail.

Continuation of Jenny Lake Loop

A footbridge crosses Cottonwood Creek by the East Shore Boat Dock. Cottonwood Creek flows south and collects tributaries from Moose Ponds, Glacier Gulch, and Bradley and Taggart lakes before joining the Snake River.

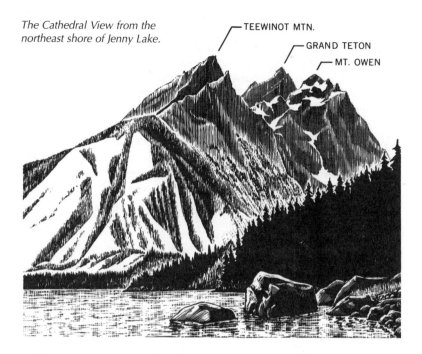

The Cathedral View from the northeast shore of Jenny Lake.

TEEWINOT MTN.

GRAND TETON

MT. OWEN

The trail continues almost 2.5 miles along the east shore of Jenny Lake with marvelous views of the Tetons. Teewinot Mountain (Shoshone for "many pinnacles") rises in front of the Grand Teton and hides the taller mountain until it dramatically emerges near the northeast corner of the lake. At the head of Jenny Lake, the trail follows the east side of the String Lake outlet. The String Lake parking area is reached .4 miles after leaving the northeast shore of Jenny Lake.

STRING LAKE TO BEARPAW LAKE
AND TRAPPER LAKE (VIA LEIGH LAKE)

This is a good early-in-the-season hike because the snow melts from this trail even while it still covers the mountains. The trail provides good views of the mountains, and the track is wide and level. Even in the summer this hike is a good choice for a valley walk, since it offers many of the same views as Jenny Lake Trail but is not as crowded. Also, backpackers with young children will enjoy this hike, since the campsites are only a couple of miles up the trail.

LENGTH: 3.7 miles to Bearpaw Lake; 4.4 miles to Trapper Lake; 7.4 and 8.8 miles, respectively, round-trip. The campsites and beach on Leigh Lake are 2.2 to 2.5 miles from the String Lake parking area.

NOTE: An easy loop hike of 3.4 miles can be made around String Lake. Follow the trail along the east side of String Lake (.9 mile). Cross the footbridge just below Leigh Lake, and hike .8 mile to Paintbrush Canyon Trail. Take that trail south, back to the west side of String Lake (1.3 miles), then hike north (.4 mile) along the outflow from String Lake back to the parking area.

DIFFICULTY: This hike is flat and is rated *easy*. Only twice does the trail climb 40 or 50 feet up the moraine then back down. In some places the trail is wide enough for two hikers to walk abreast.

ELEVATION: 6,800 feet with little variation.

ACCESS: From Moose Entrance Station, drive 11 miles north on Teton Park Road to North Jenny Lake Junction. Turn left and follow the signs to String Lake parking area. Turn right and drive to the northern end of the parking area. The trailhead is immediately north of the parking area.

NOTE: In summer, this parking area fills quickly, so start early in the morning to get a space.

MAP: Leigh Lake and Jenny Lake, page 44.

Mount Moran as seen across upper String Lake.

TRAIL DESCRIPTION: The trail enters a lodgepole pine forest with an understory of huckleberry and false huckleberry and runs north along the shore of String Lake. Grouse whortleberry and heartleaf arnica also find room to grow along the path. Botanists like this trail because it offers some relatively uncommon plants (for example: alder, laurel, and limber pine) within easy walking distance.

In early summer, kinglets and vireos can easily be heard singing. But one song stands out above the others: the ascending flute-like notes of the Swainson's thrush.

Early morning hikers can search the far lakeshore for deer and elk. Moose and bears also visit the lake. A careful approach to the water's edge will often reveal trout or whitefish in the shallow waters.

Unlike the other Teton lakes formed by terminal moraines, String Lake is shallow and has a sandy bottom. The water warms quickly in summer, and the long, narrow lake is popular with swimmers and canoeists.

The trail forks after .8 mile at the north end of String Lake. The left fork goes to Paintbrush Canyon Trail, while the right fork follows the eastern shore of Leigh Lake.

A short walk leads up onto the terminal moraine of Leigh Lake. This moraine was deposited by the two glaciers flowing down Paintbrush and Leigh canyons. Leigh Lake is 250 feet deep in places. Like other lakes lying at the base of the Teton Range, the deepest part of Leigh Lake is along its western edge rather than in the middle. The reason for this phenomenon is the continuing sinking of the valley at the Teton Fault: The floor of the valley slopes down to the west, and the bottoms of the lakes follow true to form.

The Teton Mountains from the east shore of Leigh Lake.

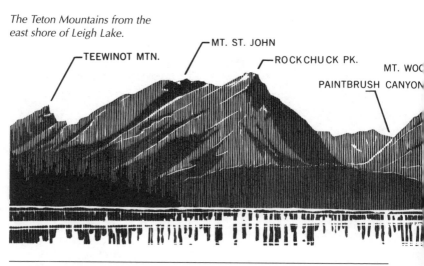

MT. ST. JOHN

TEEWINOT MTN.

ROCKCHUCK PK.

MT. WOC

PAINTBRUSH CANYON

Next the path comes back down from the moraine and parallels the shoreline closely. Sometimes spotted sandpipers may be seen on the little islands just off shore. Mergansers may be found swimming near shore, and ospreys soar above the lake looking for fish.

After a little more than 2 miles from the String Lake parking area, the trail comes to the beach and camping area on the east shore of Leigh Lake. Here the lake is shallow and has a sandy bottom, creating one of the best swimming holes in the park.

Directly across the lake are three large mountains: from left to right, Rockchuck Peak, Mount Woodring, and Mount Moran. (A rockchuck is the western version of a woodchuck, or a marmot.) Paintbrush Canyon lies between Rockchuck Peak and Mount Woodring, and Leigh is the next canyon to the north between Mount Woodring and Mount Moran. Several canoe-in campsites are located at the mouths of Leigh and Paintbrush canyons. They require a free backcountry camping permit.

The dark diabase dike running vertically through Mount Moran is quite visible from this viewpoint, as is Falling Ice Glacier. A thin layer of limestone at the top of Mount Moran is all that is left of thousands of feet of sedimentary rock that have been eroded from the top of the mountain.

At the foot of Rockchuck Peak is an easily visible fault scarp. Here the Teton Fault runs just above the glacial moraine. The scarp reveals just how much the valley has fallen and the mountains have risen since the glacier deposited the moraine.

In 1981, lightning started a fire on Mystic Isle near the north end of Leigh Lake. The fire jumped to the mainland and spread north to the shores of Jackson Lake, burning 2,500 acres before snows extinguished it.

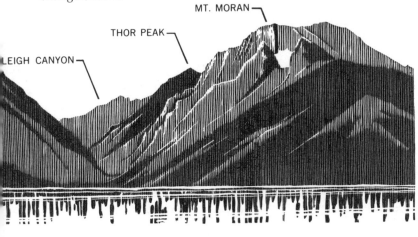

MT. MORAN

THOR PEAK

LEIGH CANYON

The trail enters the burn near the northeast corner of the lake. Burns and the insects they attract make good habitat for woodpeckers and flycatchers. Grasses (usually the first plants to regenerate), flowers and young lodgepole pines grow profusely in the burn. A "doghair forest", or extremely thick lodgepole stand (see **Hermitage Point**, page 97), seems to be getting a good start in much of the burned area. Counting the growth whorls (layers of branches) on the tallest of these young trees reveals the number of years that have elapsed since the fire. Usually, one year of growth is represented by each whorl.

Soon after the trail passes the patrol cabin on the left, it forks. The trail to the right is a short walk down to Bearpaw Lake with its marshy habitat. Continuing straight leads to Trapper Lake. This trail fades away from the burn through a low sagebrush meadow and past the west side of Bearpaw Lake. The area around these two lakes seems to be a favorite for crossbills, small seedeaters with fantastically adapted bills. Often they perch on the tops of conifers.

Trapper Lake lies at the foot of Mount Moran in a unique area where several habitats come together: the lake, a small willow marsh, a morainal forest, and mountain meadows. Two very inviting camp-sites are perched just above Trapper Lake.

CASCADE CANYON
(including forks to Hurricane Pass and Paintbrush Divide)

The beauty and accessibility of Cascade Canyon make it a very popular hiking area. Taking a shuttle boat across Jenny Lake eliminates 2 miles each way from the Jenny Lake parking area to the Cascade Canyon Trailhead. After steeply climbing to the canyon entrance, the trail settles into a gentle ascent through the spectacular lower canyon.

Cascade Canyon is a classic U-shaped, glacially sculpted canyon with a spacious floor and high, steep walls of metamorphic rock. Avalanches and the eroding forces of water continue to shape the canyon.

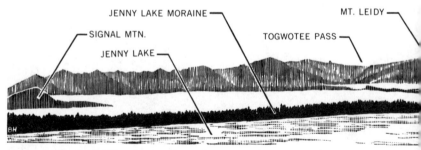

Jackson Hole and the Gros Ventre Mountains as seen from Inspiration Point.

The scenery is unsurpassed, and the flowers and wildlife offer plenty of diversion. Harlequin ducks nest along Cascade Creek. Early in the morning and late in the day, moose may sometimes be seen browsing in the shrubs along the creek. Black bears are also present, and the hiker should be constantly vigilant.

The hike up Cascade Canyon to Hurricane Pass offers many sub-alpine and alpine treats, including Schoolroom Glacier with its text-book geologic features. This fork is also much less traveled than the trail leading to Lake Solitude.

The trail that follows the north fork of Cascade Creek continues past Lake Solitude and on to Paintbrush Divide. This trail is more heavily traveled because of the popularity of Lake Solitude and the connection with Paintbrush Canyon. The Cascade/Paintbrush loop is 19.2 miles.

LENGTH: From the West Shore Boat Dock to Inspiration Point is .9 miles one way. To the forks of Cascade Creek is 4.5 miles one way (add 1.7 miles to one-way distances if hiking from String Lake parking area, and add 2 miles from Jenny Lake parking area).

From the Cascade Creek forks to Hurricane Pass is 5.1 miles one-way. To Paintbrush Divide is 5.1 miles one-way (subtract 2.4 miles if Lake Solitude is the destination).

DIFFICULTY: These hikes are rated *difficult* because of their length and elevation gains. The trails afford good footing, although some of the steeper portions are rocky. The switchbacks up to Hurricane Pass lead through scree and can be slippery. The same is true of the hike to Paintbrush Divide. Snow remains on the upper portions of these trails until late June or early July. Check with park rangers for trail conditions.

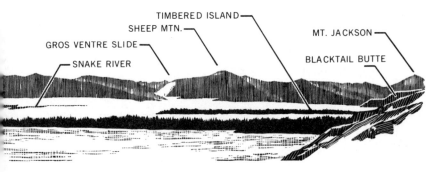

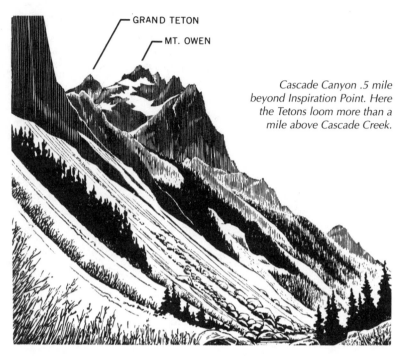

GRAND TETON

MT. OWEN

Cascade Canyon .5 mile beyond Inspiration Point. Here the Tetons loom more than a mile above Cascade Creek.

ELEVATION: Jenny Lake lies at 6,783 feet. Inspiration Point is a little more than 400 feet higher (7,200 feet). The forks of Cascade Creek sit at about 7,800 feet, a gain of only 600 feet over 3.6 miles of trail. Hurricane Pass and Paintbrush Divide each lie 2,600 feet higher at 10,400 feet. Lake Solitude lies at 9,035 feet.

ACCESS: From Moose Entrance Station to Grand Teton National Park, drive 6.8 miles to the South Jenny Lake parking area. Follow signs to the East Shore Boat Dock.

NOTE: In mid-summer, the parking area fills up. Starting early in the morning will usually assure a space.

MAP: Lupine Meadows to Leigh Lake, page 38.
Leigh Lake and Jenny Lake, page 46.
Inspiration Point Inset, page 47.

TRAIL DESCRIPTION: From the Jenny Lake parking area, you can take the boat shuttle across Jenny Lake and save 2 miles of walking around the south end. The boat shuttle operates in the summer months. Call (307) 733-2703 for the current schedule and rates. A description of the 2 mile walk is given in the **Jenny Lake Loop** section.

From the West Shore Boat Dock, follow the signs to Cascade Canyon. The nearby peaks are made of metamorphic rock, and large gneiss boulders with granite intrusions lie along the trail. This area is frequently used for practice by rock climbing schools.

From the boat dock to Hidden Falls and Inspiration Point is one of the most popular hikes in the park. If heavy foot traffic is encountered, don't be tempted to leave the trail. Shortcutting causes erosion and is dangerous. Instead, you may want to take some time to look in the creek for dippers which are small, slate-colored birds that can be found anywhere along the creek below the falls. They feed in fast-moving mountain streams by actually walking under the water and picking insect larvae off rocks.

A huge Engelmann spruce marks the intersection of the Valley Trail. Pikas often are seen poking in and out of rocks on the rocky slope near the intersection. The trail continues to the right and affords an opportunity to admire the imposing face of Storm Point. One-half mile from the boat dock there is a 50-yard spur leading to an excellent spot to view Hidden Falls.

The trail crosses Cascade Creek and continues climbing to Inspiration Point, a popular destination for many hikers. There are several spots along this steep portion of the trail that are only 5 feet wide, with 40- or 50-foot drops over the edges. These areas are dangerous only when hikers are not paying attention. Be careful with small children, and don't wear slippery shoes.

The views from Inspiration Point are impressive with Jenny Lake stretching out below. The moraine impounding Jenny Lake is quite visible from this perspective. The view east across the valley includes Sleeping Indian Mountain and the Mount Leidy Highlands. The view west features Mount Owen and Teewinot Mountain.

NOTE: Since Hidden Falls and Inspiration Point are the most popular hiking destinations in Grand Teton National Park, the trail from the West Shore Boat Dock to Inspiration Point is sometimes jammed with hikers. Ranger-led groups are also conducted to these destinations. This can be slow and frustrating for hikers continuing up Cascade Canyon. There are two ways to avoid this congestion.

1. Be at the East Shore Boat Dock for the first shuttle, and beat the crowds.

2. North of the West Shore Boat Dock, a secondary trail climbs directly to Cascade Canyon Trail, joining it west of Inspiration Point. Though intended for horse use, few horses actually use the trail. If you want to avoid the crowds and catch Hidden Falls and Inspiration Point on the way down, when fewer hikers are on the trail, this may be an alternative.

About .5 mile beyond Inspiration Point, the trail enters the canyon and leaves the valley behind. The grade is quite moderate, gaining only 200 to 300 feet over the next few miles.

The trail starts off through thimbleberry bushes and meets the horse trail coming in from the right. Silky phacelia and columbine appear at the entrance to the canyon.

For the next few miles, the trail alternately crosses open boulder fields, flower-filled meadows, and cool forests of mixed conifers with an understory of serviceberry, honeysuckle, and mountain ash (plants that like the shade and the acidic soil found under conifers). Marmots and pikas scamper among the huge, glacier-transported boulders. Listen for thrushes in the woods and warblers in the willows near the stream.

The uphill grade is almost unnoticeable in the lower canyon. The canyon floor is expansive, surrounded by towering peaks and a diverse mixture of habitat. Small stands of large Douglas firs give off a wonderfully fresh smell.

Mount Owen (12,424 feet) is recognizable by its sharp spires and multiple snow fields. Valhalla Canyon cuts to the south behind Mount Owen. Soon the Grand Teton will appear, loom larger and larger, and eventually dominate the south wall of the canyon.

The continuing geologic story is made evident by avalanche chutes and rock falls. A large eroded bank watches over dead trees that no longer have soil to support them. Marvelous monkshood grows along the trail.

After crossing the footbridge over Cascade Creek, the trail begins to get steeper. At 4.5 miles from the boat dock, the trail forks. To reach Lake Solitude, take the right fork (skip the following description of **South Fork of Cascade Canyon to Hurricane Pass** and read instead **Cascade Canyon to Lake Solitude**. To hike to Hurricane Pass, continue reading.

SOUTH FORK OF CASCADE CANYON TO HURRICANE PASS

This trail is not heavily traveled and has much to offer the hiker in scenic grandeur, flowers, and geology. It gains 2,600 feet in 5.1 miles and is usually snow free by the middle of July.

At the beginning of South Fork Trail, a high cascade plunges on the right, and the eastern ridge of Table Mountain looms above. Two rock walls enclose the cascade. Aside from the Parry primrose growing among the boulders near the water, the south wall doesn't appear much different from the rest of the canyon. The north wall, on the other hand, is striking. Red paintbrush and yellow groundsel contrast starkly with the shiny black rock. The flat surface of the wall looks as if someone took a giant knife and cleanly sliced it. The black rock forming the wall is schist, a metamorphic rock that often splits into large, flat plates.

Above the cascade the trail becomes steeper and bends to the right, providing a snapshot view of the valley in the distance. Raucous Steller's jays sometimes fly from tree to tree in the mixed conifer forest. Brook saxifrage and speedwell grow along the seeps, and gooseberry and baneberry form the understory. On the left, the Grand Teton now pops above the closer peaks to the south. The trail crosses and recrosses the creek.

In early summer, every turn in the trail seems to produce a new flower: globeflower, marsh marigold, tofieldia. The seeps and springs along the trail support their own natural rock gardens of moss, ferns, and flowers. Two miles after entering the South Fork, the trail winds through a stand of very large whitebark pines.

Just after entering the South Fork camping zone, the trail breaks into the open. Avalanche debris clutters the floor of the canyon. The trail switches back at a large rock outcropping, presenting a 360-degree view of mountain peaks. Several large avalanche chutes are visible, as is the Grand Teton.

The flowers get more varied and more numerous: mountain bluebells, columbine, marsh marigolds, Parry primrose, and elephanthead. Blooming buttercups and spring beauties early in the summer show that snow has not been gone very long. The dominant tree at this elevation is whitebark pine.

The prominent peak to the west of the South Fork Trail is Table Mountain.

A large red avalanche chute is visible on the south wall. The pink granite appears to be less impervious to water than the rock around it. This would account for the weakness in the wall that developed into a large funnel.

Bird life is noticeably different at this altitude. Spotted sandpipers may be found on the ponds in the high meadows. Bluebirds, nutcrackers, solitaires, and hermit thrushes inhabit the small stands of trees. Swallows fly above and rock wrens sing from the cliffs. Ravens and golden eagles may sometimes be found soaring high above. Now you can start looking for pipits, rosy finches, and other alpine species.

After the area designated for horse camping, the trail cuts through debris created by a recent avalanche. Heather and dwarf mountain laurel line the trail.

Soon Avalanche Divide Trail branches off to the left. This trail climbs to the divide between Avalanche and Cascade canyons (1.6 miles), running up to the base of the Wall, an impressive cliff formed of layers of ancient limestone. Avalanche Canyon drops from the other side of Avalanche Divide. (This can be hiked, but there is no maintained trail.)

South Fork Trail continues straight for 1.3 miles to Hurricane Pass and soon begins switching back up through snow fields. The Grand, Middle, and South Tetons dominate the view to the east. Moss campion can be found among the rocks near the trail. This small, pink cushion plant takes 100 years or more to grow to the size of a dinnerplate. The switchbacks may be tiring, but they offer the chance to admire many wildflowers, including mountain sorrel, ivesia, bistort, alpine pussytoes, and townsendia.

The Wall from the trail's end at the Cascade-Avalanche Divide.

Before making its final assault on Hurricane Pass, the trail winds gently through high mountain meadows, continuing the transition between subalpine and alpine. Schoolroom Glacier is straight ahead. The cirque of this once enormous ice mass can be seen expanding far to the right and left.

Now the trail begins to climb up the steep dolomite cliffs of the cirque. The path is made of limestone scree, so be careful. Above the camping zone, many more wildflowers put on an impressive show: phacelia, western wallflower, anemone, townsendia, thistle milkvetch, green gentian, sky pilot. Fields of yellow polka dots—buttercups— enliven the view below.

This is the place to get a close look at a glacier. Schoolroom Glacier is a classic glacier in miniature with many features plainly visible: the bergschrund (where the ice has pulled away from the headwall); crevasses; lateral moraines; a terminal moraine which has been broken through in the middle; and a small, impounded lake resting in a scooped-out basin.

Just before the pass, a view to the west reveals the gradual sloping of the Tetons on that side of the range. Compare this with the precipitous eastern slope caused by the Teton Fault.

At Hurricane Pass the trail reaches 10,400 feet—well above tree line. Dwarf alpine flowers abound : forget-me-nots, Parry lousewort, buttercups, and hymenoxys. To the north, Mount Moran lies beyond Table Mountain. To the east, of course, the three Tetons continue to dominate the view.

Hurricane Pass is 9.6 miles from the West Shore Boat Dock and 11.6 miles from the Jenny Lake parking area. From here, a trail leaves Grand Teton National Park, enters the Jedediah Smith Wilderness, and continues on to Alaska Basin (see **Alaska Basin**).

CASCADE CANYON TO LAKE SOLITUDE

From the confluence of Cascade Creek with its south fork, the trail leads to the right, following Cascade Creek 2.7 miles to Lake Solitude. Beyond the lake, the trail climbs 2.4 miles to Paintbrush Divide and joins Paintbrush Canyon Trail. Lake Solitude lies at 9,035 feet, a gain of 1,235 feet from the trail's junction with South Fork Trail. Paintbrush Divide lies almost 1,400 feet higher than Lake Solitude.

The Cascade Canyon hikes penetrate the heart of the Tetons. This is the portion of mountain range that has been most uplifted by geologic pressures. All of the sedimentary rock has been worn away by erosive forces of wind and water, leaving only walls of metamorphic rock flanking the north branch of Cascade Canyon.

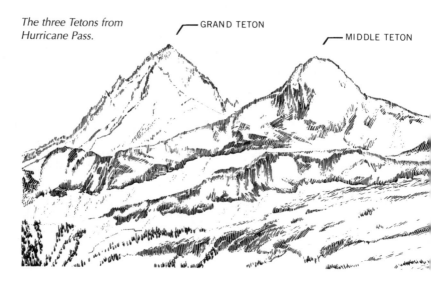

The three Tetons from Hurricane Pass.

GRAND TETON

MIDDLE TETON

The hike along the north fork of Cascade Creek offers interesting geologic features, a wonderful variety of wildflowers, a chance to see some of the high country birds, and some of the park's most spectacular scenery. The trail starts off through a lodgepole pine forest. Before long, spruce and fir trees replace most of the pines. One Engelmann spruce growing next to the path on the left is in excess of 5 feet in diameter. The forest floor is covered with a variety of shrubs, including mountain ash and gooseberry, and a variety of wildflowers including arnica, showy (purple) daisies, groundsel, parrots-beak, goldenweed, and Engelmann asters. Just before the footbridge that crosses Cascade Creek, the Cascade Creek patrol cabin lies hidden in the woods on the left. Delicate flowers such as brook saxifrage, claspleaf twisted-stalk, and five-stamen miterwort grow under the footbridge.

The trail breaks into the open, and it becomes obvious immediately that this is a classic, U-shaped, glaciated canyon. Columbine, St. John'swort, and bistort grow among the boulders, while the meadows up the canyon are a sea of purple daisies. Gaining elevation steadily, the trail passes the 8,000-foot point, and whitebark pine trees begin to appear. Back down the canyon, the Grand Teton dominates the view.

The monoliths rising high above the western wall of the canyon are called the Wigwams. Between two of these wigwams, a wide swath of young firs descends. Willows line the drainage in the middle of this area, and mature conifers form two vertical lines on either side of the swath. Major avalanches periodically wipe out most of the vegetation in this wide chute. In the interim years, trees and other plants regain a foothold and prosper until the next avalanche.

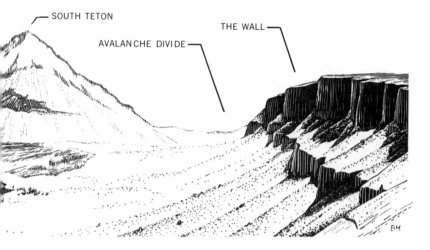

SOUTH TETON

AVALANCHE DIVIDE

THE WALL

BH

A footbridge crosses the creek again, and the trail enters the North Fork camping zone. The meadows are covered with gardens of wildflowers: paintbrush, mountain dandelion, spirea, Lewis monkeyflowers, and ubiquitous purple daisies. Lovely, bluish-purple, mountain bog gentian becomes more numerous. Mountain bluebells begin to appear near seeps trickling from the ground, contrasting wonderfully with pink spirea and fuchsia monkeyflowers. Yellow warblers and white-crowned sparrows sing from the willows. Solitaires may sometimes be seen in the taller trees.

Where there are flowers, usually there are also hummingbirds. Three different species of hummingbirds (broad-tailed, rufous, and calliope) nest in the park. Any one of the three may be visiting almost any of the flowers by the trail. Butterflies, on the other hand, seem to be a little more choosy. Many have a preferred host plant for nectaring and laying eggs.

The trail cuts through a large rockslide where marmots and pikas whistle and bleat, making sure a hiker's presence is known to all. Near the head of the canyon, the moraine that impounds Lake Solitude can be seen. Mountain bluebells, with their bluish-green leaves, line stream braids flowing down the western slope and along the bottom of the canyon. Seen from afar, the effect is somewhat mesmerizing: the streams seem to widen, seeps look like creeks, and creeks look like rivers; and the bluebells waving in the breeze become ripples riding across the blue-green water. And the Grand Teton rises from below.

Next, the trail leaves the camping zone and begins its climb up the moraine. A dead, barkless whitebark pine reveals how some trees

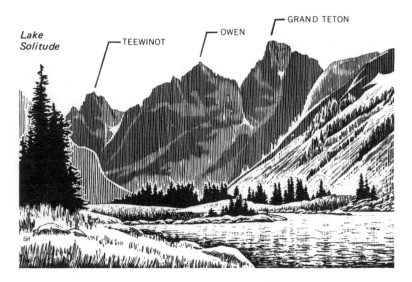

grow twisting one way then the other, becoming stronger and more able to withstand the harsh conditions of higher altitudes. Also in this area are clumps of pines growing together. They may be the result of Clark's nutcrackers which gather mouthfuls of pine seeds, store them in the ground for later, and sometimes forget to come back for them.

Lake Solitude lies behind the moraine at an elevation of over 9,000 feet. Trees are rather sparse around the lake, but heather, elephanthead, snow cinquefoil, bistort, and glacier lilies thrive in the moist, subalpine soil. Even though there are fewer birds at this elevation, pipits, bluebirds, rosy finches, or even a golden eagle may be seen.

The head of the canyon is a giant, classic cirque sculpted by a glacier that must have been a sight to behold. The top of the cirque is devoid of fossil-containing sedimentary rock. The only rock seen in these walls is the ancient, igneous variety.

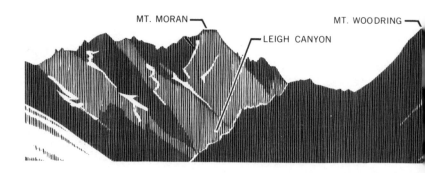

LAKE SOLITUDE TO PAINTBRUSH DIVIDE

To ascend to Paintbrush Divide, the 2.4 mile trail follows a series of steep switchbacks through loose rock. This section of trail affords sweeping views that include green, jewel-like Mica Lake to the west and the Grand Teton to the south. Craggy peaks surround Paintbrush Divide (10,700 feet), while massive Mount Moran dominates the view to the north.

PAINTBRUSH CANYON TO PAINTBRUSH DIVIDE

Paintbrush Canyon faces north, so Paintbrush Divide, which separates Paintbrush and Cascade canyons, does not become free of snow until late in the summer. Holly Lake, a cirque lake, is a popular destination for hikers, and is described below. The Paintbrush-Cascade loop also attracts hikers interested in a long day hike or a one-night backpacking trip.

LENGTH: 6.2 miles to Holly Lake; 7.9 miles to Paintbrush Divide via Paintbrush Canyon; 19.2 miles for the Paintbrush-Cascade loop.

DIFFICULTY: The trail to Holly Lake is steadily uphill, but becomes steepest in the last mile before the lake. This section of the trail is rated *moderate to difficult*. From Holly Lake to Paintbrush Divide, the steep trail climbs 1,300 feet in 1.7 miles and is considered to be *difficult*.

ELEVATION: Holly Lake is at 9,410 feet; Paintbrush Divide lies at 10,700 feet.

ACCESS: Park at the String Lake Trailhead for the Paintbrush-Cascade Canyon loop. To hike to Holly Lake, park at either the Leigh Lake Trailhead or the String Lake Trailhead, both of which are located on a spur road that leaves Jenny Lake Scenic Drive.

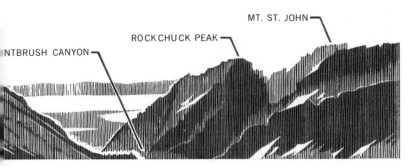

View to the east from Paintbrush Divide.

The North Fork and the Tetons from the Paintbrush Divide Trail.

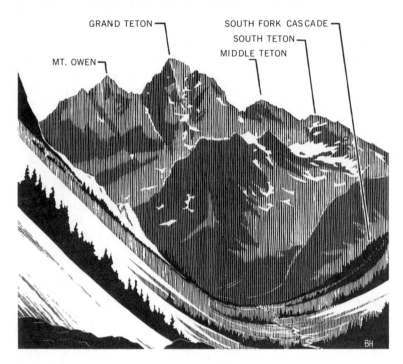

GRAND TETON ─┐   SOUTH FORK CASCADE ─┐
SOUTH TETON ─┐
MIDDLE TETON ─┐

MT. OWEN ─┐

BH

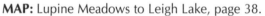

MAP: Lupine Meadows to Leigh Lake, page 38.

TRAIL DESCRIPTION: The approach to Paintbrush Canyon is through about 2 miles of conifer forest. The trail from String Lake Trailhead first crosses the creek-like lake, then leads south for .3 mile to the junction with Paintbrush Canyon Trail which heads northwest from this junction along the spine of a glacial moraine.

The lower Paintbrush camping zone begins in the conifers. When the trail breaks out of the trees, there is a panoramic view of lower Paintbrush Canyon. During summer, the wildflower display in the open part of the canyon attests to its being aptly named. During early fall, the leaves of shrubs and wildflowers splash colors up the sides of the canyon.

The trail climbs steadily up, then crosses boulder fields on the north side of the canyon before switching back up to subalpine meadows and the junction with the trail to Holly Lake. The spur trail to Holly Lake first passes the group/horse campsite, then leads to Holly Lake, a gem of a glacial tarn nestled against the south side of Mount Woodring.

From Holly Lake, an unmarked trail opposite the trail to the Holly Lake campsites leads 1.7 miles to Paintbrush Divide. First the trail traverses a rocky meadow with scattered small stands of whitebark pine and subalpine firs. To reach the divide, the trail leaves trees behind at the Upper Paintbrush camping zone and switches back steeply uphill through scree which is often covered with snow throughout the summer. Paintbrush Canyon at 10,700 feet provides spectacular mountain views in all directions. Mount Moran dominates the view north.

Holly Lake and Rockchuck Peak.

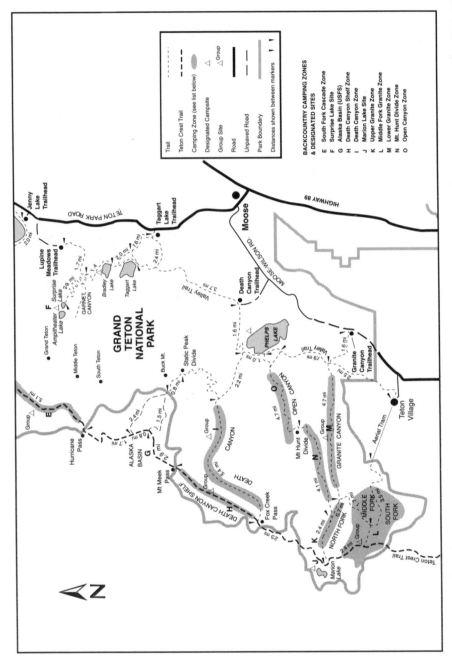

TETON VIILLAGE TO LUPINE MEADOWS MAP

SOUTH TETON TRAILS FROM
LUPINE MEADOWS TO TETON VILLAGE

VALLEY TRAIL
(Teton Village to Lupine Meadows parking area)

The Valley Trail traverses the hilly moraines at the foot of the Tetons and spans 15.8 miles from Teton Village to the Lupine Meadows parking area.

A number of parking areas for intersecting trails provide access to various segments of the Valley Trail without having to walk its entire length. Portions of the Valley Trail may also be used to make loop hikes. The entire trail can be hiked easily in a long day.

One of the best hikes to explore Jackson Hole's forested moraines, the Valley Trail lies mostly in mixed conifer forests (lodge-pole and limber pine, subalpine and Douglas fir, and Engelmann spruce). Occasionally it opens into small meadows or into aspen stands where birds and wildflowers are prevalent. The trail runs on or near the Teton Fault, skirts three piedmont lakes, and cuts across the Taggart Lake burn.

LENGTH: From Teton Village
> to Granite Canyon Trail Junction—2.5 miles
> to Open Canyon Trail Junction—4.4 miles
> to Death Canyon Trailhead—7.5 miles (Whitegrass Patrol Cabin)
> to Beaver Creek Trail Junction—10.9 miles
> to Taggart Lake Trail Junction—11.6 miles
> to Amphitheater Lake Trail Junction—14.1 miles
> to Lupine Meadows parking area—15.8 miles

DIFFICULTY: The full Valley Trail hike is rated *moderate-to-difficult,* primarily because of its length. Most of the hills are relatively small, but considering the overall elevation changes, the *moderate-to-difficult* rating is called for. The trail is well marked and affords good footing.

ELEVATION: The trail begins near Teton Village at 6,440 feet and ends at Lupine Meadows at 6,760 feet. The highest points of the trail peak at Phelps Lake Overlook (7,200 feet) and at the intersection with Amphitheater Lake Trail (7,400 feet). There are many hills along the way, so you will gain and lose several hundred feet on a number of occasions.

ACCESS: Hiking the entire Valley Trail requires setting up a shuttle between your starting and ending points.

To get to the access points on the southern portion of the trail, drive south on the Moose-Wilson Road that originates across from the Grand Teton National Park Visitor Center in Moose. From Moose, the mileages to the different access points are as follows:

TETON VILLAGE—Drive south 8 miles. Turn right and drive .3 miles to the parking area. Walk past the tram tower, then go right toward the last ski lift. You should see the Jackson Hole Ski Corporation office and a buck-and-rail fence with signs for Grand Teton National Park boundary and the Valley Trail. Follow the white arrows up the hill where there should be a sign at the entrance to the Valley Trail. (At the time this book was written, there was construction in this area, and getting to the Valley Trail was confusing. If directions are not clear, ask for help at the ski corporation office.)

GRANITE CANYON—Drive south 5.9 miles. Pull into the parking area on the right. From the parking area, hike 1.5 miles to the Valley Trail intersection and gain about 250 feet in the process. The trail starts off through a sagebrush field and then follows the edge of an aspen stand.

It climbs through an open field with numerous wildflowers up onto a moraine where the conifer forest begins.

DEATH CANYON TRAILHEAD (WHITEGRASS PATROL CABIN)—Drive south 3 miles. Turn right and drive about 2 miles to the parking area. Start from the Death Canyon Trailhead and walk about 100 yards to the junction with the Valley Trail.

To get to access points for the northern portion of the Valley Trail, enter Grand Teton National Park at the Moose Entrance Station. From this entrance, the mileages to the access points are as follows:

TAGGART LAKE—Drive 2.5 miles to the Taggart Lake parking area on the left. See **Taggart Lake Loop** for a description of the two trails leading to their intersections with the Valley Trail. From the trailhead at the parking area, it is a few hundred yards to where the trail forks. The left branch extends about 1.5 miles to the Valley Trail intersection at Beaver Creek. The right branch extends about 1.4 miles to the Valley Trail intersection at Taggart Lake.

LUPINE MEADOWS PARKING AREA—Drive 6.5 miles and turn left. Follow signs to the parking area (about 2 miles). The trailhead for Amphitheater Lake Trail and the northern terminus of the Valley Trail lie at the end of the parking area.

MAP: Teton Village to Lupine Meadows Area, page 66.

TRAIL DESCRIPTION: After parking in Teton Village, walk to the chair lift at the far north end of the ski area and follow the signs to the Valley Trail. The route leads up onto a moraine, a climb of about 350 feet from the village floor. Several unofficial trails cross the main trail. After going through a conifer forest, the trail enters an open area with several small aspen stands. Wildflowers cover the open areas and birds may be heard singing. The trail then enters a conifer forest before intersecting Granite Canyon Trail in 2.4 miles.

The trail remains relatively flat for the next mile, and then climbs about 350 feet before reaching the Open Canyon Trail intersection (a total of 1.7 miles from the Granite Canyon intersection). In another .4 mile, the Valley Trail meets a trail from the left. This is the cutoff for hikers coming from the Death Canyon Trail who want to reach the Open Canyon Trail.

The Valley Trail continues past Phelps Lake, up to Phelps Lake Overlook, and then on to the Death Canyon Trailhead (Whitegrass patrol cabin), a distance of about 3.4 miles.

Near Phelps Lake the trail crosses Death Creek, the kind of fast-moving stream preferred by American dippers. Ferns, clematis, columbine, and other plants normally associated with shaded areas grow in open, sunny areas near the creek's inlet to Phelps Lake. These plants require moisture but not necessarily the shade that preserves moisture. Glacial till at the bottom of the moraine, saturated with water draining into Phelps Lake, provides the moisture these plants need.

The Valley Trail leaves Phelps Lake and begins a gradual climb through an open meadow. On sunny days, snakes sometimes sun-bathe on glacially deposited boulders near the trail. (Snakes are cold blooded and need sun to warm them so they can attend to their daily activities.) Grand Teton National Park has no venomous snakes, but along this section of trail nonvenomous garter snakes can be spotted. The only other snake found in the park is the rarely seen rubber boa, a small constrictor that kills its prey with muscles rather than venom.

About .5 mile from Phelps Lake, the Valley Trail joins the Death Canyon Trail coming in from the left. The trail continues to Phelps Lake Overlook, and climbs the south face of the moraine as it switches back across a large wildflower meadow. During late spring and summer, this slope is ablaze with flowers including giant hyssop, balsamroot, little sunflower, and groundsel. Serviceberry and Rocky Mountain maple grow next to the trail.

Phelps Lake Overlook is an ideal place to relax and enjoy the view. Two large lateral moraines and a smaller terminal moraine left

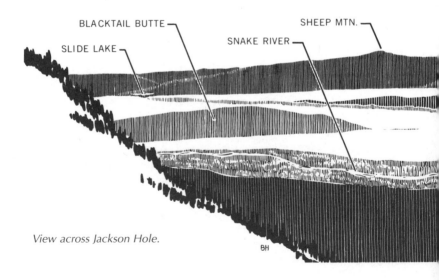

BLACKTAIL BUTTE

SLIDE LAKE

SHEEP MTN.

SNAKE RIVER

View across Jackson Hole.

BH

by the Death Canyon Glacier impound this deep clear lake. The private J-Y Ranch is nestled at the east end of the lake.

The trail switches back down a lateral moraine formed by Death Canyon Glacier. It traverses the head of a gulley and enters a stand of large Douglas firs. The moraine includes the higher ridge to the south and the nearby gulley which was scooped out of the moraine by either an avalanche or a wash. The trail approaches an aspen stand where Lazuli buntings nest and corn lilies and geraniums grow.

Continuing down the moraine, the trail enters a dry open area with pink geraniums. Later, the trail enters a damp forest of subalpine fir and Engelmann spruce. Geraniums here are white and prefer a moist environment. (When geraniums are blooming, look for little lines on petals leading to the center of the flower. The lines act as nectar guides for insects—a sort of welcome mat to expedite dispersal of pollen.) The trail crosses a small stream with cow parsnip, coneflowers, and alder blanketing the nearby forest floor.

Where the forest changes to lodgepole pine, warblers and thrushes may be heard singing; coralroot, false Solomon seal, bog orchids, ferns, and monkshood may be seen growing on the damp forest floor; and huckleberry, thimbleberry, and honeysuckle share the understory with Rocky Mountain maple and shade-tolerant, young subalpine firs. Even though the mature forest is dominated by lodgepole pines, young lodgepoles prefer more sunny, open areas. The trail reaches Death Canyon Trailhead 4.9 miles after leaving the Granite Canyon Trail intersection.

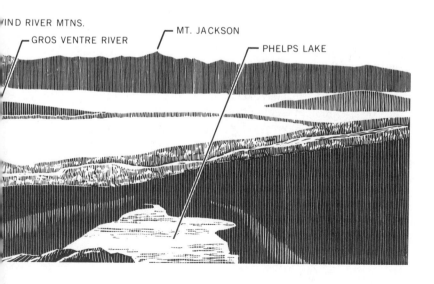

WIND RIVER MTNS.

GROS VENTRE RIVER

MT. JACKSON

PHELPS LAKE

From Death Canyon Trailhead, the Valley Trail hike to the north is relatively flat (about 6,800 feet). It traverses 3.3 miles on a terminal moraine to the Beaver Creek Trail Junction.

The trail enters a mixed woodland of lodgepole pine, aspen, and Douglas fir. Continuing north, the track bisects a small burn and winds through mixed woods, including a small stand of very large aspens, and open meadows. Accipiters (woodland hawks) may be seen hunting along the ridge to the west while woodpeckers, tanagers, and vireos inhabit the forests flanking the trail. The intersection with the Beaver Creek Trail provides a good view of the Taggart Lake burn.

From the Beaver Creek Trail Junction to Bradley Lake is about 2 miles. The trail climbs up and down lateral moraines on the sides of Taggart and Bradley lakes.

After crossing Beaver Creek, the trail follows the edge of a thick conifer forest next to the burn. The trail emerges from the forest into the burn and switches back to the top of the morainal ridge south of Taggart Lake. Flycatchers, including olive-sided, may be seen and heard throughout the burn. Young lodgepole pines represent the generation of trees that will succeed the fire. The trail then descends to the lake, crosses a footbridge over Taggart Creek, and soon forks. The right fork leads to the Taggart Lake parking area (1.6 miles).

The left fork, heading north, is a continuation of the Valley Trail and leads 1.1 miles to Bradley Lake. The trail climbs over the moraine that separates Taggart and Bradley lakes. Shortly after reaching Bradley Lake, the trail forks. The right branch returns to Taggart Lake Trail (.9 mile), rejoining it 1.1 miles from the parking area.

The Valley Trail continuation on the left branch heads north from Bradley Lake 1.4 miles to Amphitheater Lake Trail junction. Bradley Lake lies at 7,022 feet. A footbridge crosses a small strait connecting two lobes of the lake. The trail climbs through a mixed forest about 400 feet onto a moraine and then crosses a meadow before intersecting with the Amphitheater Lake Trail.

The elevation at this intersection is about 7,400 feet. The Valley Trail then descends about 700 feet over the next 1.7 miles to its terminus at Lupine Meadows parking area. A variety of woodland birds (including woodpeckers, flycatchers, thrushes, tanagers, and owls) inhabit the area between the intersection and the parking area. See **Lupine Meadows to Amphitheater Lake** section for a description of this portion of the Valley Trail.

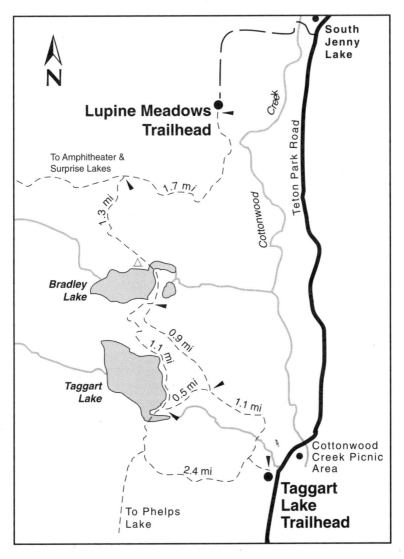

TAGGART LAKE LOOP

In the dry summer of 1985, a lightning fire burned an area of over 1,000 acres between Beaver and Taggart creeks and around Taggart Lake. The loop takes the hiker through the burn and adds the dimension of a firsthand opportunity to view the natural succession of plant and animal life.

The trail leads from the parking area through a sagebrush meadow and up onto the burned moraine. Hikers are treated to a variety of wildflowers, birds, and mammals as forest regeneration is well underway. Taggart and Bradley lakes were named by F. V. Hayden for Frank Bradley and W. Rush Taggart, chief geologist and assistant geologist of Hayden's 1872 expedition to the Tetons. The lakes are impounded by moraines deposited by glaciers that flowed out of Avalanche and Garnet canyons.

This loop hike is not difficult. Although the hike is popular, it is not nearly as well traveled as the hikes around the Jenny Lake area. The relatively short hike through the burn presents many interesting features not found on most other hikes.

LENGTH: From the parking area, it is 2.4 miles to Taggart Lake via the Beaver Creek arm to the south. The return to the parking area via the Taggart Creek arm to the north is 1.6 miles, making the loop hike 4 miles. The hike can be lengthened another 1.5 miles (5.5 miles total) by adding the Bradley Lake loop.

DIFFICULTY: The hike is rated *easy to moderate*. One fairly steep hill gains about 350 feet in altitude. The trails are well marked, and footing is fairly good in most places.

ELEVATION: The Taggart Lake parking area is at about 6,600 feet. Taggart and Bradley lakes lie at 6,902 feet and 7,022 feet. The trail climbs up to 7,120 feet on the lateral moraine south of Taggart Lake and then to that height again on the moraine between the lakes.

ACCESS: From the Moose Entrance Station, drive north about 2.7 miles on the Teton Park Road. The Taggart Lake parking area is on the left.

MAP: Taggart Lake Trailhead, page 73.

TRAIL DESCRIPTION: The trail leaves the parking area, cutting through a sagebrush meadow filled with balsamroot, gilia, groundsel, lupine, and Indian paintbrush. Halfway through the meadow, a little bridge crosses a stream. Calliope hummingbirds often nest in the willows near the bridge. Early in the morning, elk sometimes may be seen grazing in the meadow to the south.

At the foot of the moraine, the trail forks and creates a loop. The south fork follows the edge of the burn where young lodgepole pine trees have gained a solid foothold. This tree's cone is ideally suited to

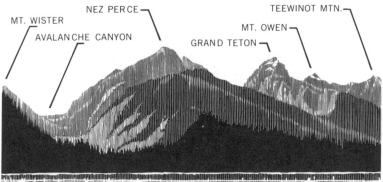

surviving forest fires. The heat from a fire will open a cone's scales and trigger the release of the cone's seeds. Lodgepole pine seedlings prefer sunny, open areas. Because of this preference and the lodgepole's unique cone structure, these pines usually are the first trees to thrive after a fire. By counting the clusters or whorls of branches on the tallest of the new trees, you can determine the number of years since the fire.

The trail soon heads into the burn and begins climbing onto the moraine. Flycatchers and woodpeckers inhabit burns and often may be seen among the charred trees. A loud alarm whistle of a marmot may be heard, and sometimes these "rockchucks" may be seen scampering among the rocks. Many wildflowers, including geraniums, larkspur, and harebells, grow near the trail.

Following the rim of the moraine, the trail turns west near Beaver Creek. Moose may be seen browsing in the willows below. Warblers and flycatchers nest there. The trail descends to the creek and enters an unburned stand of aspens and conifers. Numerous large animal trails filled with the tracks of ungulates (hoofed mammals) cross the path, so you should stay alert for moose walking to or from the marshy lowlands.

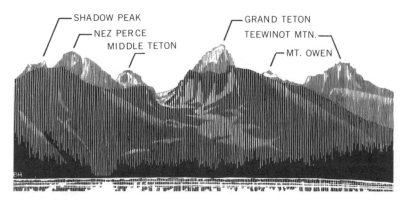

After 2.4 miles, the trail is joined by the Valley Trail from the left. The trail continues near the edge of a thick conifer forest and emerges from the forest into the burn, switching back to the top of the morainal ridge south of Taggart Lake. A dense stand of young lodgepole pine flourishes in the sediment of an old lake atop the moraine. It will soon become a "doghair forest" with trees growing as thick as the hairs on a dog's back. These trees were not planted but grew from seeds that germinated after the fire.

The trail then descends to the lake, crosses a footbridge over Taggart Creek, and soon forks. The left fork is a continuation of the Valley Trail and leads 1.1 miles to Bradley Lake. This trail climbs over the moraine separating Taggart and Bradley lakes. Shortly after reaching Bradley Lake, the trail forks. The right branch returns .9 mile and joins the Taggart Lake Trail 1.1 miles from the parking area.

The right fork leads back to the parking area (1.6 miles), following Taggart Creek through the burn. Purple asters, fireweed, groundsel, and sticky geranium highlight a lush carpet of green grasses. Spreading dogbane and snowbrush ceanothus may also be found along the trail. The trail turns south at the bottom of the moraine, crosses Taggart Creek, and then cuts through the sagebrush meadow near the parking area.

TRAILS FROM RENDEZVOUS
MOUNTAIN SKI TRAM

The Jackson Hole Ski Area is located in Bridger-Teton National Forest, adjacent to Grand Teton National Park. The aerial tram provides year-round transport to the top of Rendezvous Mountain—10,450 feet above sea level and 4,150 feet above the valley floor. The tram affords quick access to the alpine zone and the Teton Crest Trail and Granite Canyon Trail without having to climb the mountain. From the tram, the Rendezvous Mountain Trail leads to both these trails. It is also possible to hike up or down Rendezvous Mountain along the ski corporation's service road.

While hikes in this area offer many features of alpine hikes farther north in the Tetons, one obvious difference is the origin of the rocks forming the mountains. Trails from Rendezvous Mountain present many views of nearby cliffs formed of limestone and dolomite rock layers. Fossils in these strata reveal life-forms from the periods when they were deposited.

Trails in the north, on the other hand, wind their way through mountains revealing only igneous and metamorphic rock—granite, schist, and gneiss. Being higher, these mountains to the north have been more vulnerable to the forces of erosion and have been stripped of sedimentary rock. (The northern portion of the Teton Range is higher than the southern Rendezvous Mountain area for two reasons: geologic forces produced greater uplift along that portion of the Teton Fault, and the southern area subsided along other faults that run more or less perpendicular to the Teton Fault.)

After leaving the tram at the top of Rendezvous Mountain, a walk to the top of the knoll just west of the tower will provide a panoramic view. Far to the north the Grand Teton is visible. Immediately to the north lies Granite Canyon. To the east are Sleeping Indian and the Gros Ventre Range. Construction and development are evident in the view of the valley below. (Fortunately, Ninety-seven percent of Jackson Hole lies either in Grand Teton National Park or Bridger-Teton National Forest and cannot be further developed.) Mountains and cliffs to the south and west dramatically reveal layers of sedimentary rock deposited millions of years ago when vast inland seas covered the area.

NOTE: The tram takes only 12 minutes and is an easy way to get into the high Tetons. It's especially convenient for hikers carrying heavy backpacks.

LENGTH: From the top of the aerial tram
to the Middle Fork Cutoff—3.5 miles.
to the Granite Canyon Trail Junction—5.2 miles.
to the Valley Trail Junction (via Granite Canyon Trail)—9.9 miles.
to Granite Canyon parking area—11.6 miles.
to Teton Village (via Valley Trail)—12.7 miles.
to Teton Crest Trail Junction (via Middle Fork Cutoff)—4.1 miles.
to the North Fork of Granite Canyon Trail Junction—5.5 miles.
to Marion Lake—6.3 miles.
to Fox Creek Pass—8.9 miles.
to Teton Village via the ski area service road—7.4 miles

DIFFICULTY: These trails are rated *difficult* because of their length and elevation changes. The tram can eliminate an initial climb of over 4,000 feet. Even with that, the hiker should be fit and be able to handle the challenges of a long hike with frequent gains and losses in elevation.

The trails are well marked and offer good footing most of the time, except in areas with scree.

ELEVATION: The top of the tram sits at 10,450 feet. The trail to the Middle Fork Cutoff (8800 feet) is mostly downhill. From this cutoff, the trail to Marion Lake (9,200 feet) climbs up and down fairly steep pitches, netting a gain of 400 feet in the process. From the Middle Fork Cutoff, the trail down Granite Canyon to the Valley Trail loses about 2,000 feet fairly steadily.

The trail down the ski area service road is all downhill and loses 4,100 feet of elevation. The trail is fairly steep in places and is sometimes covered with scree. The scree can be slippery on many of the steep downhill pitches.

ACCESS: Teton Village and the Granite Canyon Trailhead are both reached from Grand Teton National Park's Moose Visitor Center by driving south on the Moose-Wilson Road, which originates across the highway from the visitor center. From Moose, mileages to different access points are as follows:

TETON VILLAGE—Drive south 8 miles. The aerial tram is located next to the village parking area.

GRANITE CANYON—Drive south 5.9 miles to the Granite Canyon parking area. From the parking area, hike 1.5 miles to the intersection with the Valley Trail and gain about 250 feet in the process. The trail leads through a sagebrush meadow then follows the edge of an aspen stand. It then climbs through an open meadow filled with numerous wildflowers up onto the moraine where the conifer forest begins.

MAP: Teton Village to Lupine Meadows Area, page 66.

TRAIL DESCRIPTIONS: The top of the tram is slightly above the tree line and thus is in the alpine zone. Ivesia, Townsendia, hymenoxys, alpine forget-me-nots, and many other alpine wildflowers may be found growing along the trail. Krummholz, or stunted versions of whitebark pine and Engelmann spruce, bend away from the direction of the prevailing wind.

TO THE MIDDLE FORK CUTOFF AND
TO GRANITE CANYON TRAIL

The trail leads down the slope to the south. Shaded somewhat from wind, silky phacelia, sulphur paintbrush, phlox, sweetvetch, and flax grow near the path. At the intersection, the trail's left fork descends the mountain on the ski area service road (see **Aerial Tram to Teton Village**, page 82). The right fork, Rendezvous Mountain Trail, leads to the Granite Canyon Trail. Just beyond the intersection, to the left, is a large boulder of sedimentary rock distinguished by its cover of orange lichen. The lichen grows very slowly, breaking down the rock into soil. Telesonix saxifrage may be seen growing in the cracks of this rock.

A sign announces the way to Marion Lake and Granite Canyon and the boundary of Grand Teton National Park. Look for mountain bog gentian, moss campion, and cinquefoil growing along the trail. Twisting to the north, the trail begins a descent of the east wall of a large cirque, known as the Bowl. Layers of dolomite and limestone form the cliffs guarding the rim of the cirque. Wind, funneling up this bowl, creates harsh growing conditions for plants. The trail leads down through a forest of growth-stunted spruce trees. Across the basin, the trail may be seen climbing the west wall of the cirque.

Farther north along the trail where the wind is less of a factor, the trees are much larger and the forest is fairly open. Snow lingers late here, and other than a few flowers (elephanthead, parrots-beak, and showy daisy), there is little ground cover. The trail switches back, and soon you are again in a windy funnel with growth-stunted trees. Flowers grow in abundance among the rocks in the moist soil of this slope.

The trail crosses the cirque's basin through mountain bog gentian, elephanthead, and willows growing among the rocks. Wrens and sparrows sometimes drink from small pools of water.

The west wall of the cirque displays marvelous gardens with incredible numbers of flowers—Engelmann asters, geranium, paint-brush, flax, penstemon, groundsel, showy daisies, columbine, dunce-cap larkspur, and fireweed.

The trail climbs out of the bowl and affords views of some of the most beautiful flower-filled meadows in the park. It crosses a ridge and then switches back down through a forest of Engelmann spruce and enters the Middle Fork camping zone. This is the closest camping zone to the tram, but campers should be aware that water is limited here, especially late in the summer as many small streams dry up. About .5 mile after entering the zone, there are a couple of fairly permanent streams. Mountain bluebells and brook saxifrage grow in profusion along their banks.

The dense spruce/fir forest gives way to open stands of subalpine fir. Small flower-filled meadows host butterflies and hummingbirds. The Middle Fork Cutoff is 3.5 miles from the tram. From this junction to the Teton Crest Trail is .6 mile, or you can stay on the Rendezvous

Mountain Trail to reach the Granite Canyon Trail in 1.7 miles.

The Rendezvous Mountain Trail descends through wildflower-filled meadows to Granite Canyon. The west side of Rendezvous Mountain appears barren due to pounding by the elements. Natural erosion is taking place so rapidly that little vegetation becomes established.

Nearing Granite Canyon, the trail enters a dense coniferous forest, leaves the camping zone, and crosses two footbridges over the North and Middle forks of Granite Creek. Upstream from the first bridge, the creek tumbles over shelves of sedimentary rock. The beautiful little cascade creates a moist, mossy environment. A patrol cabin may be seen to the left after the trail crosses the second bridge. At the next trail junction, the Granite Canyon Trail leads left .7 mile to the Open Canyon Trail Junction and 1.8 miles to the Teton Crest Trail Junction. The trail down Granite Canyon is to the right. From this intersection, it is 4.7 miles to the Valley Trail, 6.4 miles to Granite Canyon parking area, and 7.5 miles to Teton Village (via the Valley Trail).

The trail follows Granite Creek on the north slope of the canyon and soon enters Lower Granite Canyon camping area. The lower canyon snows melt relatively early, allowing snowfree backpacking earlier in the season than other canyons. The trail enters an old spruce/fir forest with an understory of mountain ash, gooseberry, and other shrubs. Rocky Mountain parnassia, monkshood, brook saxifrage, and pyrola grow among the moss-lined rivulets tumbling down the mountainside.

As the trail opens a bit, the north face of Rendezvous Mountain is visible across the canyon. Sedimentary layers slanting down to the west suggest some of the dynamics of the Teton Fault: Looking south toward Rendezvous Mountain, the valley lies to the east. As the valley slipped, the mountains were pushed up along the plane of the Teton Fault. The layers of rock at the top of Rendezvous Mountain were level when deposited. Now the east side of Rendezvous Mountain, pushed higher than the west side, reveals more evidence supporting the theory of the Teton Fault (see **Geology of Jackson Hole**, page 13).

The opposite side of the canyon also displays enormous avalanche chutes. Although Granite Canyon has the classic U-shape of a glaciated canyon, the very bottom appears to be V-shaped. This might suggest avalanches, rock and mud slides, and other forces related to water and gravity that have been hard at work on this canyon in the few thousand years after the glacier receded.

A couple of miles down the canyon, the trail descends to Granite Creek and cuts through a boulder field. Redosier dogwood grows along the creek. Raspberries, which ripen in July, grow among the boulders; thimbleberries and huckleberries appear farther along the trail. In September, fall colors peak; redosier dogwood leaves turn brick red, and cottonwoods have a golden glow.

Although the sedimentary rock of the upper canyon might have been misleading, the lower canyon reveals dramatically how Granite Canyon got its name. High granite walls across the canyon dwarf everything.

Vegetation in the lower canyon is thick and tall. Cow parsnip and duncecap larkspur plants grow as high as 6 to 8 feet. Baneberry and elderberry try to close in on the trail. Even giant hyssop and fireweed seem to grow taller here.

Before entering a Douglas fir forest, the valley below can be seen through the mouth of the canyon. The trail gets steeper, thrushes sing in the moist forest, and you leave behind the camping zone.

The intersection with the Valley Trail is 1.6 miles from the Granite Canyon parking area and 2.5 miles from Teton Village. Turn left at the intersection to take the Valley Trail to the north. Turn right and the trail soon comes to another intersection. Here the Valley Trail is joined by the trail to Granite Canyon parking area (1.5 miles). The trail to the parking area leaves the coniferous forest and descends the moraine through a wildflower-filled meadow. Continuing straight on the Valley Trail (rather than turning left to the parking area), it runs south 2.4 miles to Teton Village. This is not the most pleasant segment of the Valley Trail—it is heavily traveled by horses, and it is confusing. Still, there are flowers and birds along the way.

On the confusing segment to Teton Village, every time a horse trail comes in from the left, it should be ignored. The Valley Trail continues straight south. Near the end of the trail, there are two signs. The older sign directs the hiker to go straight to Teton Village, but the newer directs the hiker to take the fork to the right. The trail following the newer sign eventually emerges onto one of the ski slopes well above Teton Village.

MIDDLE FORK CUTOFF TO FOX CREEK PASS
(via Teton Crest Trail and Marion Lake)

This hike offers rolling meadows of subalpine wildflowers stretching in every direction. Islands of whitebark pine, subalpine fir, and Engelmann spruce trees dot the meadows, and bands of sedimentary rock form occasional horizontal rock outcroppings.

The trail joins the Teton Crest Trail .6 mile west of the Middle Fork Cutoff. The remaining 2.1 miles to Marion Lake is on the Teton

Crest Trail, which leads north and drops gently down to cross the Middle Fork of Granite Creek and then ascends a ridge before dropping down to cross the North Fork of Granite Creek. The last .5 mile to Marion Lake is uphill, but the reward for the steep ascent is a tiny jewel of a lake tucked up against a limestone wall. The wildflower meadows around Marion Lake are especially lush in the summer.

From Marion Lake to Fox Creek Pass, the aptly named Teton Crest Trail ascends to the park boundary and enters Targhee National Forest. Then the trail passes to the west of Spearhead Peak and re-enters Grand Teton National Park at Fox Creek Pass. This 2.3 mile section of trail crosses alpine meadows of ground-hugging cushion plants with views of Idaho farmland to the west of the Tetons.

AERIAL TRAM TO TETON VILLAGE
(via the ski area service road)

At 10,450 feet, the top of Rendezvous Mountain lies at or above the tree line. Alpine flowers such as forget-me-nots, hymenoxys, cinquefoil, and buttercups cover the ridge along the top of the mountain and blanket the broad expanse of Rendezvous Bowl (the first mile of trail switches back down this bowl). In Jackson Hole, this is the easiest place to find rosy finches and American pipits in the summer. The shrill whistles of marmots and sharp bleats of pikas may be heard coming from the rocky meadows. This trail offers a panoramic and unsurpassed view of the valley and the southern Teton Range.

The hike down the mountain winds its way along the edges of spectacular sedimentary cliffs. The trail traverses wildflower-filled meadows and crosses mountain seeps and streams. It cuts through stands of whitebark, limber, and lodgepole pine, Douglas and subalpine fir, Engelmann spruce, and quaking aspen. An astonishing variety of birds may be seen during the descent. Mammals sometimes seen from the trail include moose, deer, elk, black bears, porcupines, marmots, pikas, squirrels, chipmunks, and weasels.

Many signs of human activity can be seen during this hike—roads and buildings in the valley, ski lifts, a restaurant (open only during ski season), machines and equipment near the trail—and quite a few people. It is difficult to get the feeling of isolation or of truly being in the mountains on this hike, but there is a lot to see, and, whether hiking up or down the trail, you'll get a good workout.

HIKES FROM DEATH CANYON TRAILHEAD

ACCESS: The trailhead is located near the Whitegrass patrol cabin at an altitude of 6,800 feet. The parking area is at the end of Death

Canyon Trailhead Road, a spur road running 2 miles west from its intersection with the Moose-Wilson Road and climbing about 350 feet in the process. To get there, coming from the south, drive north on the Moose-Wilson Road 5 miles from the Teton Village turnoff. Coming from the north, drive south on the Moose-Wilson Road 3 miles from its intersection with the Teton Park Road (just across the highway from the Moose Visitor Center). No motorhomes or trailers are permitted on the Moose-Wilson Road or at Death Canyon Trailhead.

Death Canyon Trailhead offers two options. Hiking north on the Valley Trail to Beaver Creek Trail (3.3 miles) is one. The other serves as the shortest route to Death and Open canyons. The trail leading off to the south (or left) is the section of the Valley Trail that takes the hiker to the Phelps Lake Overlook and then to the intersection of the Death Canyon and Open Canyon trails.

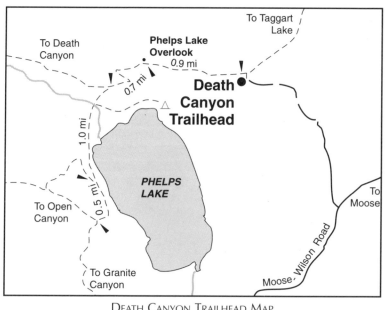

DEATH CANYON TRAILHEAD MAP

DEATH CANYON TRAILHEAD TO THE INTERSECTIONS OF OPEN CANYON AND DEATH CANYON TRAILS

Whether you intend to climb up through one of the canyons or you just want to take a short walk up to Phelps Lake Overlook and back, this section has much to offer: An abundance of wildflowers and shrubs, a variety of birds, and some impressive scenery all are part of this hike.

LENGTH: The hike to the Phelps Lake Overlook is .9 mile each way. The Death Canyon and Open Canyon Trail junctions are 1.6 and 2.6 miles, respectively, from the trailhead.

DIFFICULTY: This hike is rated *moderate*. Most of the walk up to Phelps Lake Overlook is uphill. None of this section is steep, however, and the trail offers good footing. From the overlook to the intersection with Death Canyon Trail (.7 miles), the trail descends by way of three long, steep switchbacks. The downhill portion of the hike is easy, but it can be rather disheartening if you return this way after a long day hike, because the return trip, obviously, involves a steep uphill hike.

Death Canyon Trail Junction to Open Canyon Trail Junction is 1 mile. The trail climbs rather steeply near the end of this section.

ELEVATION: The walk up to the overlook from the trailhead represents an elevation gain of about 400 feet. The descent to Death Canyon Trail intersection loses 400 feet. The continuation to Open Canyon Trail Junction first loses about 100 feet and then climbs about 300 feet before the intersection.

The trailhead lies at 6,800 feet; Phelps Lake at 6,633 feet; Phelps Lake Overlook at 7,200 feet; Death Canyon Trail Junction at 6,800 feet; and Open Canyon Trail Junction at 7,000 feet.

MAP: Death Canyon Trailhead, page 83.

TRAIL DESCRIPTION: In the beginning this trail rises gently through a lodgepole pine forest. Warblers and thrushes may be heard singing, and the birding can be good—but the wildflowers can be even better. Coralroot, Solomon seal, bog orchids, ferns, and monkshood may be seen growing in the damp forest floor. Huckleberry, thimbleberry, and honeysuckle share the understory with Rocky Mountain maple and young subalpine firs. The geraniums seen here are a white species (Richardson's) that prefers the shady, damp forest. If they're blooming, the lines on the petals leading to the center of the flower may be visible. These lines act as nectar guides for insects—a sort of welcome mat this plant evolved to expedite the dispersal of its pollen.

Soon the trail crosses a small stream with cow parsnip, coneflowers, and alder blanketing the nearby forest floor. Engelmann spruce are becoming more numerous.

Continuing up the moraine, the trail enters a drier open area where sticky geranium, a pink species, prefers a sunnier, drier environment. Lazuli buntings nest in the aspen stand nearby.

The trail progresses up the lateral moraine formed by Death Canyon Glacier. This moraine includes the higher ridge to the south. The nearby gulley lying in between, was scooped out of the moraine by an avalanche or a wash. The trail enters an aspen stand where corn lilies and white geraniums grow. At the head of the draw, the trail enters a stand of large Douglas firs, and a short walk farther brings you to the Phelps Lake Overlook. Two large lateral moraines and a smaller terminal moraine left by the Death Canyon Glacier impound this clear, deep lake. At the far end nestles the private J-Y Ranch.

After leaving the overlook, the trail switches back down across the south face of the moraine, which is mostly a large wildflower meadow. During late spring and summer, this field is ablaze with flowers including giant hyssop, balsamroot, little sunflower, and groundsel. Serviceberry and Rocky Mountain maple grow next to the trail.

The trail forks 1.6 miles from the trailhead. To go to **Death Canyon**, take the trail to the right and read the description below. To go to **Open Canyon**, continue left on the Valley Trail for another mile until you reach the Open Canyon Trail Junction (see description below).

The Valley Trail continues downhill toward Phelps Lake. On sunny days, snakes sometimes sunbathe on glacially deposited boulders near the trail. Snakes are cold blooded and need sun to warm them up so they can carry on their daily activities. Grand Teton National Park has no venomous snakes. You might see nonvenomous garter snakes. The only other snake that is found rarely in the park is the rubber boa, a small constrictor that kills its prey with muscles instead of venom.

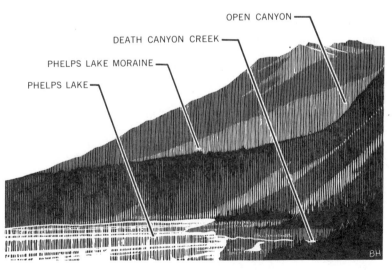

OPEN CANYON

DEATH CANYON CREEK

PHELPS LAKE MORAINE

PHELPS LAKE

BH

Near Phelps Lake the trail crosses Death Creek, a fast-moving stream of the type preferred by American dippers. Ferns, clematis, columbine, and other plants normally associated with shaded areas grow there in the open, sunny spots near where Death Creek empties into Phelps Lake. What these plants really want is moisture and they do not necessarily need the shade that preserves it. Glacial till at the bottom of the moraine is saturated with water draining into Phelps Lake and provides all the moisture these plants need.

The trail switches back up through a Douglas fir stand and at 2.6 miles comes to Open Canyon Trail. The Valley Trail continues straight to Granite Canyon Trail. The trail to Open Canyon branches to the right.

OPEN CANYON TRAIL TO MOUNT HUNT DIVIDE AND GRANITE CANYON TRAIL

This trail is not one of the park's most popular. It's a 3 mile hike before you really begin to get back into the mountains. Also, many hikers don't like the idea of having to climb up the Phelps Lake switchbacks after hiking all day. But the canyon's relative inaccessibility becomes one of its strengths—there aren't many people in Open Canyon.

The scenery, flowers, and wildlife are comparable to most canyons, but the geology may be more interesting than most. This is not a typical U-shaped canyon showing many effects of glaciation. Open Canyon instead owes its existence to two other geologic forces—a fault system running perpendicular to the Teton Fault, and the erosional forces of running water.

This hike may be best for those who have explored most of the other canyons and are looking for something new and different.

LENGTH: 4.7 miles from Open Canyon Trail Junction to Mount Hunt Divide; 4.1 miles additional to continue to Granite Canyon Trail Junction; 1.2 miles additional to Teton Crest Trail Junction.

DIFFICULTY: This hike is rated *difficult.* The trail climbs steadily uphill to Mount Hunt Divide with some fairly steep sections. The next section of trail going to Granite Canyon Trail Junction slowly but steadily loses altitude. The final section to Teton Crest Trail has a steady altitude gain. The trail is well marked and, after snows are gone, permits good footing.

ELEVATION: The Open Canyon Trail Junction lies at 7,000 feet. The

Mount Hunt Divide rests at 9,710, an altitude gain of 2,700 feet. The Granite Canyon Trail Junction lies at 8,400 feet, a loss of 1300 feet. The Teton Crest Trail Junction lies at 8,900 feet, a gain of 500 feet.

MAP: Teton Village to Lupine Meadows Area, page 66.

TRAIL DESCRIPTION: The trail at first follows a knife-like ridge, a lateral moraine pushed up by glaciers on both sides. It then climbs along the lower slopes of Prospector's Mountain. Huckleberry bushes make up the understory of the mature lodgepole pine forest. When the berries are ripe, be on the alert for bears. Soon a spur from the Valley Trail comes in from the left. Open Canyon Trail continues to the right.

The trail cuts across a southwest-facing meadow with huge Douglas firs and many flowers. In early summer, beautiful leopard lilies bloom. This flower's face opens downward, thus it loses less pollen to rain. The flies that pollinate these flowers have no problem reaching the inner parts of the flower from below.

Just before Open Canyon Creek, avalanche damage is obvious near the trail. Subalpine fir trees 2 feet in diameter are found broken off 15 to 20 feet above ground. A major avalanche in 1986 cleared large areas in the canyon and opened it up for future avalanches. Great quantities of debris litter the canyon. A bridge crosses the creek a few yards upstream from a large Engelmann spruce with a subalpine fir huddled against it. Somehow these trees withstood the momentum of the avalanche. A high waterfall cascades from the cliffs, and, in early summer, columbine and silky phacelia may be seen blooming near the bridge.

The trail crosses the creek and climbs the south side of the canyon through a spruce/fir forest. This moist, north-facing slope supports a relatively dense undergrowth of huckleberry and honeysuckle. The trail continues climbing through a very tall spruce forest and occasionally crosses avalanche chutes. Snow lingers in these chutes, which support different and later blooming vegetation.

Sometimes the trail opens. The relatively dry south-facing slope across the canyon supports only sparse vegetation. Fingers of trees come down the slope in small ravines that hold enough water to support these plants.

The trail eventually breaks out of the forest and continues up the south slope of the canyon. Many of the boulders and rocks near the trail are limestone. At first glance, this may seem puzzling since the Tetons generally are thought to be formed of metamorphic rock. In fact, across and on up to the head of the canyon, the canyon walls are metamorphic; only at the very top of those walls can sedimentary rock be seen. Yet, on the south side of the canyon, all of the rock is limestone, a sedimentary rock. These clues reveal that Open Canyon tracks an ancient fault line.

Long ago this side of the canyon and mountains to the south began falling down the fault plane. As the southerly end of the Teton Range sank, the sedimentary layers were relatively protected from the forces of erosion, even as most of the sedimentary rock at the top of the Tetons to the north eroded away. To find the same level of Precambrian rocks on the south side of the canyon as is seen on the north side would require digging more than 2,000 feet below the canyon floor!

This fault caused rock on both sides of the canyon to part company over a period of millions of years. Rock along the fault line crumbled and became subject to forces of water and gravity, resulting in a V-shaped canyon opened up by large volumes of water washing rocks and gravel downward. And yet, glaciers must also have played some part. Just after the trail emerges from the conifer forest, a careful scan of the north side of the canyon with binoculars should reveal large, smooth rock surfaces with grooves and scrapes carved by powerful ice movements.

The trail continues to switchback higher under sedimentary rock cliffs. Steep meadows are filled with wonderful columbine blooming in late June and July. Down the canyon, Phelps Lake and Blacktail Butte look familiar in the distance.

Early in summer, north-facing slopes still have snow fields. The pink color of "watermelon snow" is caused by algae growing in the snow. Remember not to eat the snow! None of the water or snow in the mountains should be consumed without filtering or boiling.

Turning to the south, the trail runs the last half mile up to Mount Hunt Divide. At 9,700 feet, there are few trees. Alpine flowers at the divide include thistle milkvetch, Townsendia, and largeflower hymenoxys. While most alpine wildflowers are small, the aptly named hymenoxys is a large flower among many smaller varieties. It is a treat to see an alpine meadow filled with these flowers just after sunrise. Stand with your back to the sun: All the blossoms will be bending at the stem and facing the east as if begging for inspection.

Few birds inhabit the area, but rosy finches, ravens, or white-crowned sparrows may be seen. Marmots inhabit the rocks, even at this altitude, and cliffs and hills to the west offer one of the best chances in Grand Teton National Park to see bighorn sheep.

To the north lies Prospector's Mountain. Rendezvous Mountain and the Jackson Hole tram can be seen to the south. And, far to the east, is a good view of the Gros Ventre Mountains.

The trail continues 4.1 miles before intersecting with Granite Canyon Trail, losing about 1,300 feet of elevation along the way. At the intersection, the hiker can take the Granite Canyon Trail left 5.4 miles to the Valley Trail or right 1.1 miles to the Teton Crest Trail.

DEATH CANYON TRAIL TO FOX CREEK PASS

LENGTH: 2.2 miles from the intersection with the Valley Trail to the junction with the trail to Static Peak Divide; 5.4 miles additional to Fox Creek Pass. A total of 9.2 miles from Death Canyon Trailhead to Fox Creek Pass.

DIFFICULTY: This hike is rated *difficult* because of its length and the elevation gains.

ELEVATION: The junction of Death Canyon and Valley trails lies at 6,800 feet. Fox Creek Pass is at 9,560 feet, an elevation gain of 2,800 feet.

MAP: Teton Village to Lupine Meadows Area, page 66.

TRAIL DESCRIPTION: From Phelps Lake, the trail heads west across a dry meadow of sagebrush and chokecherry bushes. The trail enters a stand of massive Engelmann spruce before switchbacking up the north side of the canyon beneath the monolithic rock portals guarding the entrance to Death Canyon. The trail levels out and winds westward into Death Canyon.

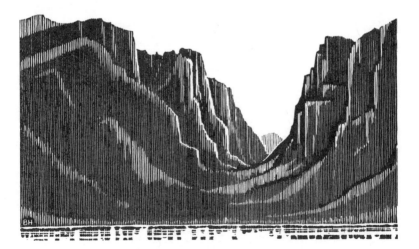

The Death Canyon patrol cabin (3.7 miles from the trailhead) is located at the junction with the trail up to Static Peak Divide. Beyond the junction, Death Canyon Trail follows the north side of a gently meandering stream flanked by tall willows. About .5 mile west of the junction, the trail crosses to the south side of the stream via two footbridges and enters the Death Canyon camping zone. From this point, the trail steadily climbs for a mile through a spruce/fir forest before emerging into open meadows dotted with huge slabs of granite. The trail follows the canyon as it curves to the southwest, and soon the upper reaches of Death Canyon come into view. Death Canyon Shelf, a layer of limestone, forms a thick horizontal white stripe on the north side of the canyon. The south side of the canyon supports dense, moist conifer forests growing where prevailing southwesterly winds allow snow to accumulate each winter.

About 3 miles west of the patrol cabin, the trail crosses to the south side of Death Creek and traverses open meadows of willows and wildflowers. Bridges span several of the minor creeks crossed by the trail. Creeks and seeps foster lush plant growth into late summer. A colorful array of wildflowers, including asters, sticky geranium, lupine, and fireweed bloom in summer on slopes at the head of Death Canyon. The trail rises out of the camping zone, switches back up the north side of the cirque to Fox Creek Pass (9,560 feet) and intersects with the Teton Crest Trail. At the pass are views of the Jedediah Smith Wilderness on the western side of the Tetons.

Meadows carpeted by ground-hugging dwarf alpine plants stretch south from Fox Creek Pass to Spearhead Peak. Marion Lake lies 2.3 miles south along the Teton Crest Trail, which takes an alpine route to reach the picturesque lake nestled in a cirque below limestone cliffs. The Teton Crest Trail follows the Death Canyon Shelf.

TETON CREST TRAIL
(Fox Creek Pass to Hurricane Pass)
TRAIL DESCRIPTION: The following description divides the stretch of the Teton Crest Trail running from Fox Creek Pass to Hurricane Pass into three segments.

DEATH CANYON SHELF AND ALASKA BASIN—Death Canyon Shelf is a wide ledge of limestone that affords unsurpassed views of the western sides of Buck Mountain and the Grand, Middle, and South Tetons. Subalpine meadows of wildflowers grow profusely along the shelf, and pikas and yellow-bellied marmots inhabit piles of loose rock.

The Death Canyon Shelf camping zone begins about 400 yards

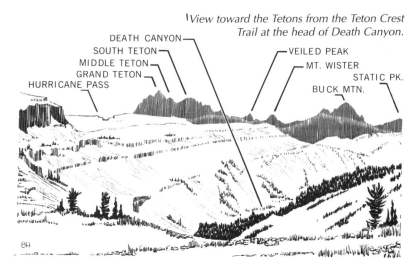

View toward the Tetons from the Teton Crest Trail at the head of Death Canyon.

DEATH CANYON
SOUTH TETON
MIDDLE TETON
GRAND TETON
HURRICANE PASS

VEILED PEAK
MT. WISTER
STATIC PK.
BUCK MTN.

from Fox Creek Pass. Stands of trees scattered along the shelf provide backpackers with foodhanging sites.

At the northeast end of Death Canyon Shelf, the Teton Crest Trail climbs to Mount Meek Pass, leaves Grand Teton National Park, and enters the Jedediah Smith Wilderness of Targhee National Forest. The Teton Shelf Trail (Targhee National Forest Trail 028) comes in from the west 500 yards from the pass. This trail leads to the Devil's Stairs (3.2 miles) and Teton Canyon campground (7 miles).

One of the Basin Lakes along the Teton Crest Trail. Buck Mountain (left) silhouetted on the skyine.

The Teton Crest Trail descends over scree fields of dolomite—a battleship gray sedimentary rock—and drops into Alaska Basin. Rock outcroppings have been worn smooth by centuries of glacial ice.

The Alaska Basin Trail (South Teton or Targhee National Forest Trail 027) intersects the Teton Crest Trail 2.9 miles from Mount Meek Pass. The Alaska Basin Trail leads east to Buck Mountain Pass, past three gem-like tarns and larger Mirror Lake nestled in a granite basin. Campsites may be found near the lakes, collectively referred to as the *Basin Lakes*, but Jedediah Smith Wilderness regulations prohibit camping closer than 200 feet from lakes and streams.

Above Mirror Lake, the Alaska Basin Trail crosses small creeks draining lush, wet meadows where white marsh marigold, pink elephanthead, and magenta Parry primrose bloom in early summer. The trail ascends and merges with a trail, the Alaska Basin Shelf Trail 026, that follows the north side of Alaska Basin. (This northern route connects with the Teton Crest Trail about 1 mile north of the Basin Lakes.) The Alaska Basin Trail leads .6 mile east to Buck Mountain Pass and the Grand Teton National Park boundary. The Alaska Basin Shelf Trail (026) leads west to Sunset Lake (2.3 miles) and Hurricane Pass (3.4 miles).

The Alaska Basin Trail passes against the southwestern flank of the summit of Buck Mountain as it climbs up to Buck Mountain Pass. A massive pile of rubble—igneous and metamorphic rock eroded off Buck Mountain—lines the trail.

The trail then ascends to Static Peak Divide (10,790 feet) with views of Jackson Hole and the Snake River below and the Gros Ventre Mountains on the east side of the valley.

STATIC PEAK DIVIDE—Steep switchbacks over loose talus lead down from Static Peak Divide. Whitebark pines, dwarfed at the divide, grow taller on the lower parts of the switchbacks. The trail crosses a saddle between Static Peak and Horace Albright Peak, then continues to descend, but the trail is not as steep. Whitebark pines are joined by subalpine firs and Engelmann spruces. The trail occasionally crosses open slopes, allowing views down to the gentle stream meandering across the floor of Death Canyon.

The trail ends at the Death Canyon patrol cabin, 4 miles from Static Peak Divide. The Death Canyon Trail heads west to Fox Creek Pass (5.5 miles) and east (3.7 miles) to the Death Canyon Trailhead.

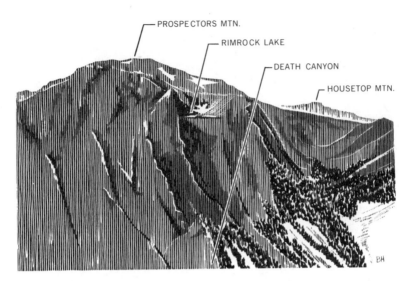

Prospector's Mountain as seen from
the Alaska Basin Trail at Static Peak Divide.

ALASKA BASIN TO HURRICANE PASS—The Teton Crest Trail leads north from the Basin Lakes to Hurricane Pass. This trail also passes Sunset Lake, a popular destination for hikers. Jedediah Smith Wilderness regulations prohibit camping near the lake, but there are several suitable campsites that are at a sufficient distance to protect the fragile habitat surrounding the diminutive glacial lake.

From Sunset Lake to Hurricane Pass the trail gains 800 feet in elevation in 1.1 miles as it makes the transition from subalpine vegetation to dwarfed alpine cushion plants.

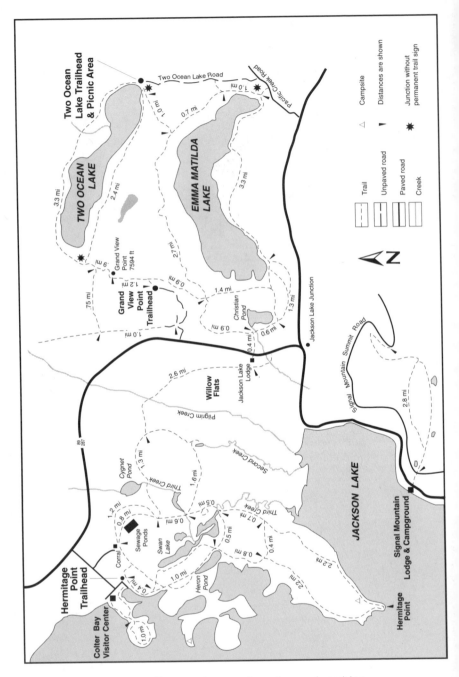

Two Ocean Lake Trailhead & Picnic Area

Two Ocean Lake Road

Pacific Creek Road

1.0 mi

1.0 mi

0.7 mi

TWO OCEAN LAKE

3.3 mi

2.4 mi

EMMA MATILDA LAKE

3.3 mi

Grand View Point 7594 ft

1.2 mi

.75 mi

2.7 mi

0.9 mi

Grand View Point Trailhead

1.4 mi

0.9 mi

Christian Pond

1.3 mi

1.0 mi

0.6 mi

Jackson Lake Junction

0.4 mi

Jackson Lake Lodge

2.6 mi

Willow Flats

Signal Mountain Summit Road

2.8 mi

Pilgrim Creek

89 287

Cygnet Pond

1.3 mi

Second Creek

1.6 mi

Third Creek

0.5 mi

1.2 mi

0.8 mi

0.6 mi

0.7 mi

Sewage Ponds

Third Creek

0.4 mi

JACKSON LAKE

Corral

Swan Lake

0.5 mi

0.8 mi

2.2 mi

Signal Mountain Lodge & Campground

Hermitage Point Trailhead

0.4 mi

Heron Pond

1.0 mi

2.2 mi

Hermitage Point

Colter Bay Visitor Center

1.0 mi

Trail

Unpaved road

Paved road

Creek

Campsite

Distances are shown

Junction without permanent trail sign

N

COLTER BAY AND JACKSON LAKE LODGE AREA MAP

NORTH TETON TRAILS FROM COLTER BAY AND JACKSON LAKE LODGE AREA

LAKESHORE TRAIL
HERMITAGE POINT (via Heron Pond and Swan Lake)
WILLOW FLATS TO COLTER BAY
TWO OCEAN LAKE LOOP (including Grand View Point)
CHRISTIAN POND LOOP
EMMA MATILDA LAKE TRAIL
SIGNAL MOUNTAIN TRAIL

LAKESHORE TRAIL

Paved sidewalks near the marina, visitor center, and amphitheater lead down to a wide, paved level trail that starts at Colter Bay Marina and goes northwest behind the visitor center to a point guarding the entrance to the bay. This walkway provides easy access to scenic views of the Tetons, with Jackson Lake in the foreground.

The remainder of the Lakeshore Trail is level but not paved; it leaves the paved section several hundred feet before its western end. The trail first winds along the edge of an open lodgepole pine forest, then crosses a dike that connects to an island forested with tall sub-alpine firs. The Lakeshore Trail mostly follows the perimeter of this island and has a few short hilly sections. The western end of the island provides expansive views of the Teton Range rising above Jackson Lake.

After recrossing the dike on the return trip, there are two ways to return to the visitor center/marina area: Retrace the original trail to the paved walkway, or head north on an unpaved trail that skirts the edge of the lake.

HERMITAGE POINT
(via Heron Pond and Swan Lake)

Most of this hike is on morainal material and glacial till deposited during the most recent glaciation that created the original impoundment of Jackson Lake. The trail takes the hiker through conifer stands and sagebrush meadows. It approaches Jackson Lake frequently and winds by several small ponds and Third Creek Marsh. Such a variety of habitats supports many birds, flowers, and mammals.

The full hike is over 9 miles but can be abbreviated to about 5 miles (or even 3). Like Willow Flats, this area can get hot in the summer and is best enjoyed early in the morning.

LENGTH: The loop hike going to the tip of Hermitage Point is 9.2 miles. The Hermitage Point Loop can be eliminated by taking a cutoff at Third Creek Marsh, saving about 4.5 miles. The hike to Heron Pond then looping back past Swan Lake is an easy 3 miles.

DIFFICULTY: This hike is rated *easy* with only a few gentle hills (less than 150 vertical feet). Maintained trails are well marked but there are several unmarked trails at Hermitage Point.

ELEVATION: 6,800 feet with less than 150 feet of variation.

ACCESS: From the Moran Entrance Station to Grand Teton National Park, continue north 4 miles on Highway 89 to Jackson Lake Junction. Bear right at this junction and stay on 89 for 5.4 miles to the Colter Bay turnoff. Turn left and follow the signs to the visitor center parking area. The trailhead itself is south of the visitor center at the end of the marina parking lot.

MAP: Colter Bay and Jackson Lake Lodge Area, page 94.

TRAIL DESCRIPTION: Hermitage Point Trailhead is at the southeast end of the marina parking lot. The lower trail initially follows the edge of the water and offers great views of Mount Moran and the Teton Range. The trail leads through a lodgepole pine forest near the water's edge. Chokecherry and serviceberry shrubs line the trail. Ospreys sometimes nest across the narrow bay on the right.

At .4 mile, the trail forks. The following description takes the path to the right and returns on the path coming in from the left (Swan Lake). Taking the right path and following the sign to Heron Pond, the trail enters a mixed wood with lodgepole pines eventually giving way to fir. At another fork, a small sign points the way to Jackson Lake Overlook. The two trails described below rejoin in about 400 yards.

The left fork goes through what is sometimes called a "dog hair forest". The lodgepoles along the trail grow as thick, seemingly, as hairs on a dog's back. They all appear to be the same age, suggesting that a disturbance of some kind leveled an earlier forest and new trees began growing thickly. This particular disturbance might have been a fire—rather than a blowdown or an insect infestation—since a fire very quickly and efficiently cleans and nourishes the forest floor. It is interesting to note that the understory of this dog hair forest is young subalpine fir. The forest is too thick for young lodgepole pines which require sunlight. Young firs, on the other hand, prefer the shade.

The right fork climbs a small hill and emerges into a sagebrush meadow with a good view of Jackson Lake and Mount Moran. The three canyons to the north of the huge massif are Moran, Snowshoe, and Waterfalls. These canyons have classic U-shaped valleys characteristic of glacial sculpting. Using binoculars, hikers can easily see Wilderness Falls (above) and Columbine Cascade (below) in Waterfalls Canyon.

The trail continues and rejoins the lower path in the dog hair forest. A few calypso orchids flower in early summer on either side of the shady, moist path as it approaches Heron Pond. Beavers inhabit this pond, and the best time to see them is early in the morning or evening. The small meadows leading down to the pond are covered with wildflowers, including gilia, harebells, asters, and lupine.

Four trails intersect at the south end of Heron Pond. To return to Colter Bay, follow the trail to **Swan Lake** (see the description at the end of this section). Continuing to Hermitage Point, the trail makes a loop. The trail described below goes to the left and follows the loop clockwise.

The left fork climbs a ridge through a blowdown of lodgepole pines. These trees are not as long-lived as some other conifers, and whole stands of lodgepoles sometimes fall victim to beetles or to wind. Woodpeckers feed on insects in the dead trees and may be seen in the area. Over the ridge, the trail descends through a lodgepole forest where trees have been used by elk to polish their antlers. Matted areas may be found where many animals have bedded down.

The trail forks at the bottom of the hill. The left fork leads through a marshy, willow-filled area providing habitat for sandhill cranes, several species of warblers, and flycatchers. The trail joins the loop trail at Willow Flats described in the **Willow Flats** section. To continue on to Hermitage Point, turn right.

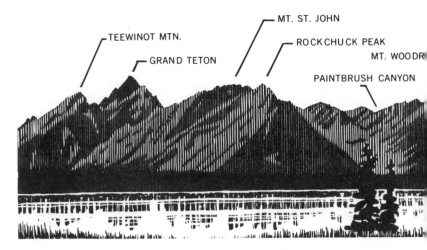

TEEWINOT MTN.

GRAND TETON

MT. ST. JOHN

ROCKCHUCK PEAK

MT. WOODR

PAINTBRUSH CANYON

The trail follows the base of the ridge and then runs adjacent to Third Creek and a willow marsh. The view over the marsh to the east includes peaks of the Teton Wilderness in the distance. Sometimes you can see raptors soaring over the marsh and moose browsing in it.

A trail joins from the right, permitting the hiker to cross through sagebrush meadows and complete a shorter loop. The main trail continues straight to Hermitage Point, leading through a sagebrush meadow then up onto a moraine, presenting a great view of Mount Moran. It continues through a mixed forest of subalpine and Douglas firs before crossing over a ridge and out into an open area. Signal Mountain lies across Jackson Lake with Mount Leidy and the Washakie Highlands beyond. The view to the west is the Cathedral Group that includes Grand Teton, Mount Owen, and Teewinot Mountain.

A little farther on is one huge lodgepole pine, a specimen tree, to the right of the trail. With no competition, this tree has done very well. Also found on this southeast-facing slope are large, thriving Douglas firs. Usually Douglas fir stands are found on relatively moist north- and east-facing slopes, but some of the largest specimens actually grow on south- and west-facing slopes. This phenomenon suggests these trees started growing during a period when Jackson Hole enjoyed more precipitation. Douglas fir cones can be readily identified by their trident shaped bracts.

Informal trails near the tip of the Hermitage Point peninsula can be confusing. The main trail stays left along the shore and presents great views of the mountains. After rounding the point, the trail returns north through open sagebrush meadows. If you look to the west, you can see Elk Island and, beyond it on the shoreline, the old Mystic

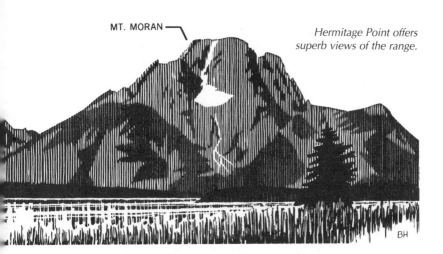

MT. MORAN

Hermitage Point offers superb views of the range.

BH

Island burn. A left fork leaves the trail and leads to Jackson Lake. The main trail continues straight, enters a forest, and comes to several depressions in the moraine that retain water in the spring and support chorus frogs. Near the depression on the right is a stand of large aspens which, requiring more moisture than some other trees, found this area hospitable. This damp environment also supports calypso orchids growing among the huckleberry and whortleberry near the trail.

The trail returns to Heron Pond and the four-way intersection of trails then continues straight for .3 mile to Swan Lake. Another great view of Mount Moran is visible from the top of the ridge running through the blowdown. Swan Lake with its yellow pond lilies waits at the bottom of the hill. Several species of ducks are usually present. The same two trumpeter swans have been living here since the early 1980s without producing any young. These birds are as bound to their territory as they are to each other, and have chased away other prospective nesters.

Finally the trail leaves the lake and passes old sewage ponds on the left. Then the trail enters a wildflower-filled meadow, where a sign directs the hiker back to Colter Bay.

WILLOW FLATS TO COLTER BAY

Hikes in the mountains are very special, but hikers looking for something different might want to try Willow Flats. Vibrant habitat and marvelous views not found on mountain trails await hikers here. In summer, midday on this trail can be hot. Hiking Willow Flats is best during the spring or fall. If you do this hike in the summer, go early in the morning or in the evening.

Since the West is dry, animals and plants tend to congregate where they can find water. Mountain streams, rivers, ponds, and lakes accommodate much wildlife. Willow Flats, an area consisting of alluvial soil deposited on an impermeable layer of rock, is one of the two largest freshwater marshes in the valley; the upper Snake River above Jackson Lake is the other. Adjacent areas of dry soil support sagebrush meadows, and scattered through the flats are islands and fingers of glacial deposits hosting mixed woodlands. These different habitats support a diverse abundance of wildlife. A bonus on this trail is the likelihood of seeing some large mammals: moose, elk, deer, and coyotes.

LENGTH: 8.5 miles. The hike can be abbreviated to 5 miles by turning around at the loop intersection or by taking a one-way hike to Colter Bay and returning by a pre-arranged shuttle (a fee is charged). Check at Jackson Lake Lodge or at the Colter Bay activities window for details on the shuttle service.

DIFFICULTY: This hike is flat and is rated *easy*; some parts are muddy in the spring. Much of the trail is a service road for the National Park Service and Grand Teton Lodge Company. Bicycles are not permitted.

ELEVATION: 6,800 feet with little variation.

ACCESS: From the Moran Entrance Station to Grand Teton National Park, continue north 4 miles on Highway 89 to Jackson Lake Junction. Bear right at this junction and stay on 89 another half mile. The Willow Flats parking area is on the left.

MAP: Colter Bay and Jackson Lake Lodge Area, page 94.

TRAIL DESCRIPTION: As you begin your hike, you will see sugarbowl (hairy clematis) and Oregon grape growing among the sagebrush surrounding the parking area. The left path leads to the overlook of the vast alluvial plain below. The Teton Range serves as a dramatic backdrop for Jackson Lake, the dam, and the great freshwater marsh. Habitat "edges" or "ecotones", which are important in nature, can be seen: sagebrush meeting marsh water, islands of aspen, and fingers of conifers. Perhaps a hawk or an eagle will be seen soaring over the marsh.

Several unofficial trails lead from the hill you are standing on to the service road below. Sandhill cranes nest in the marsh. Sparrows and warblers may be heard singing in the willows, while ground squirrels sometimes scamper along the elevated road and dike.

The service road proceeds north at the base of a hill. Exotic (non-native) plants take advantage of human disturbance, and the service road is no exception. Thistle, yellow sweet clover, and tansy grow by its side. On the left is a classic example of a beaver pond with its crescent-shaped dam and lodge. The best time to see these nocturnal animals is early in the morning or in the evening.

The slope on the right below Jackson Lake Lodge deserves more than a glance. In July and early August, brilliant scarlet gilia bloom among the sulfur buckwheat and yarrow.

Ravens have recently been using the large nest in the stand of tall aspens ahead on the left. Hikers should remain on the trail when a nest or nesting activity is observed. Birds will tolerate people walking by on regularly traveled trails, but will often abandon a nest if it is approached too closely. The hill on the right bears continued notice; just as the gilia peters out, blue penstemon and red Indian paintbrush take over. Hummingbirds may be found in this vicinity.

On another beaver pond to the right, ducks can usually be found. After the pond, willows close in on both sides of the service road. Be on the lookout for moose browsing. This section of trail is also a good place, in the fall, to hear elk bugling.

The trail next enters a mixed woodland of aspen, spruce, and lodgepole pine. The elevation gain is only a few feet, but the relative dryness of the glacially deposited soil supports a habitat completely different from the freshwater marsh. Here some of the typical wood-land birds may be seen in the stand of old-growth subalpine fir and Engelmann spruce.

The service road crosses Pilgrim Creek Bridge. At one time this was the only road to the nation's first national park. Horse-drawn car-riages and Model-T Fords must have been quite a sight as they made their way north to Yellowstone National Park. On either side of the creek, ravens sometimes sit in the tall spruce and firs, serenading each other with their hoarse croaks. Goshawks sometimes nest in the area. The females are very protective of their nest and young and will not hesitate to dive-bomb someone approaching too closely. The view of Mount Moran to the west is superb.

The trail winds its way to a relatively open area interspersed with cottonwoods and a few conifers. This is an old river terrace from Pilgrim Creek. In the fall, the cottonwoods put on an impressive yel-low show.

At 2.6 miles there is an intersection of trails . The trail now makes a 3.5 mile loop, going through a variety of habitats, and may be hiked in either direction.

Following the trail to the left soon brings you to a stand of huge cottonwoods. These giants have a cooling effect in the summer. A picnic area where Jackson Lake Lodge offers outdoor breakfasts and dinners for its guests lies to the left of the trail. In spring, pocket gopher plugs crisscross the forest floor. These mound-trails are the results of the dining forays of these small mammals: Tunneling just under the ground's surface, they eat the roots of grasses and other small plants and kick the soil up behind them.

Male butterflies flutter past, patrolling their territories. Woodpeckers and house wrens nest in the towering cottonwoods. At the edge of this deciduous stand, near the picnic area, a vast expanse of sky above the willow flats offers an opportunity to look for pelicans, eagles, and hawks soaring above and to enjoy the wonderful Teton view.

The trail soon leaves the cottonwood stand and drops just a couple of feet, bringing the hiker back to the marsh. Slightly higher "islands", where the soil is not waterlogged, support lodgepole pines. Harvester ant mounds may be found on these islands. A footbridge over Third Creek offers a view of a beaver dam and lodge on the right. A variety of ducks and shorebirds may also be seen here.

The Third Creek swamps and marshes are among the finest wildlife habitats in the park.

The next half mile may be quite muddy in the spring. The trail has become deeply rutted, collecting and holding water. Moose are seen in this area.

At the next trail junction, the loop continues to the right on the service road. The trail to the left is the connecting spur between Willow Flats and Colter Bay, described at the end of this section.

Just before the trail reaches Cygnet Pond, it passes a blowdown on the right. Here, large trees were snapped at their trunks 15 or 20 feet from the ground. The number of years since the blowdown can be estimated by counting the growth whorls (layers of branches) on the tallest young lodgepoles. Remember that one year of growth is usually represented by each whorl.

Cygnet Pond on the left may have ducks and herons and perhaps even swans. Cinquefoil and harebells grow along the trail. Crossbills sometimes frequent the tall conifers, and warblers inhabit the willows. Woodpeckers and sapsuckers nest in the cottonwoods and, late in the summer and in the fall, elk may be heard bugling.

The triangle where the two ends of this loop and the trail back to Jackson Lake Lodge come together may be confusing. Read the signs, and be sure to return on the original trail—that is, the service road running 2.5 miles back to the Willow Flats parking area.

WILLOW FLATS/COLTER BAY CONNECTION

Two roughly parallel trails lead from the Willow Flats loop to the horse corral at Colter Bay, one going past the sewage ponds and the other, a new trail, running through a variety of habitats. Hikers who have arranged a shuttle between Colter Bay and Jackson Lake Lodge can take either leg of this loop to the Colter Bay Visitor Center. These two legs are described as a 2-mile loop for those who are hiking Willow Flats and want to add these connecting trails.

From Willow Flats, the left fork of the trail leads to the sewage ponds. The trail crosses a dry area of glacial debris. Mountain bluebirds may be heard singing from the trees. Birdwatchers may find the highlight of this leg of the loop to be the sewage ponds, because ducks often come here, and shorebirds may be seen walking on or near concrete aprons around the treatment tanks. Sometimes marmots like to sun themselves on the aprons. The trail soon arrives at the corral on the right. If you want to go to the Colter Bay area, you should continue on the road past the corral.

To complete the loop, turn right at the trail running along the south end of the corral and cross the wooden footbridge. The trail climbs up the glacial ridge through the lodgepole pine forest and into a stand of subalpine fir. Young trees may be seen growing around the base of a "parent" fir. Fir cones do not fall; they disintegrate, and the seeds fall around the base of the tree forming a "fairy ring". A similar phenomenon occurs when heavy snowfall weighs down the lower branches of a fir, and new trees actually root and shoot up from the branches. Observant hikers will find examples of "fairy rings" and "snow matting".

Now the trail descends from the ridge and enters a sagebrush field. A few lodgepole pines are growing in the dry meadow. More than half of them are dead, a phenomenon typical of lodgepole. During wet years they spread into normally dry meadows. When the dry years return, many of them die, especially the younger ones that have not developed tap roots long enough to reach needed moisture.

The trail approaches another glacial ridge and continues along its base, offering a spectacular view of Mount Moran to the right. Early in the spring, chorus frogs may be heard calling from one of the ephemeral ponds in the woods.

To return to the Willow Flats parking area, turn left at the intersection with the Willow Flats trail, about 4 miles from the parking area.

TWO OCEAN LAKE LOOP
(Including Grand View Point)

About 70,000 or 80,000 years ago a glacial lobe flowed down the Pacific Creek drainage. When the glacier eventually receded, it left behind moraines that today contain Two Ocean and Emma Matilda lakes.

Two Ocean Plateau sits astride the Continental Divide. Streams draining the highlands on the plateau flow toward both the Atlantic and Pacific oceans. Two Ocean Lake, however, lies to the west of and well below the plateau and drains only to the west or toward the Pacific. Apparently somebody misnamed it.

This hike offers just about everything: flowers, birds, mammals, butterflies, scenic views, and geology. The variety of habitat includes a lake, marshes, open meadows, creeksides, mixed woodlands, and old-growth spruce/fir forests.

Even though readily accessible from two parking areas, this hike is still a bit of a secret. Away from the parking areas, few hikers are seen on the trails.

Its length makes this trail a good one-day hike. The relatively open northeast side of the lake can be warm on a sunny afternoon, so you might prefer to walk there in the morning. If the climb to Grand View Point is included in this hike, it would also be better to schedule that portion for early morning or evening—that's the best time to see large mammals in the meadows or along the lake below.

A loop can be hiked from either of two parking areas. The loop from the parking area at the north end of Two Ocean Lake Road is shorter than the loop from the Grand View Point parking area. The following description is of the longer loop: It adds a walk through an interesting forested drainage not included in the shorter loop.

LENGTH: From Grand View Point parking area (or trailhead below), 10.5 miles to hike around the lake (including returning via Grand View Point). 2.4 miles round-trip to hike to Grand View Point. From Two Ocean Lake parking area, it is a 5.8-mile hike around the lake. Add 2.8 miles (8.6 total) to include Grand View Point.

DIFFICULTY: The hike around Two Ocean Lake is rated *easy*. It's a bit long, but it's relatively flat, and the footing is good. If the steep walk up to Grand View Point is included in the hike, the rating changes to *moderate*.

Some parts of this trail are not well marked. The hiker must pay attention at all intersections.

ELEVATION: Two Ocean Lake lies at 6,896 feet. The hike around the lake is relatively flat except in one area on the southwest side of the lake where the trail gains then loses about 100 feet. Grand View Point reaches 7,594 feet, about 700 feet higher than the trail around the lake. That elevation gain takes place in about .9 mile, making the switchback hike up the mountain fairly steep.

ACCESS: To climb to Grand View Point, drive to the Grand View Point parking area. Drive 1.9 miles north from Jackson Lake Junction on Highway 89. Turn onto the unmarked gravel road that comes in from the right. This road becomes quite rough and leads to the Grand View Point parking area.

To take the hike described below, take the same gravel road, but turn left after .2 mile. Drive .1 mile and park in the area next to the trailhead.

The Two Ocean Lake parking area at the east end of the lake can be reached by driving 1 mile north on Highway 89 from the Moran Entrance Station to Grand Teton National Park. Turn right on Pacific Creek Road and drive 2.1 miles to the turnoff for Two Ocean Lake. Turn left and go 2.3 miles to the parking area.

MAP: Colter Bay and Jackson Lake Lodge Area, page 94.

TRAIL DESCRIPTION: The following description begins at the trailhead located .3 mile from Highway 89. It continues to Two Ocean Lake, runs clockwise around the lake, ascends Grand View Point, descends to the Grand View Point parking area, and returns to the trailhead. If you start at the Two Ocean Lake parking area, the descrip-

---

tion can be picked up at that point and followed according to the direction and portions of the hike chosen.

The hike starts off from the trailhead and goes through two morainal ridges. In summer, a variety and abundance of butterflies may be seen. Before long, Grand View Point looms above on the right. After 1 mile, the trail branches off to the right. There is no sign marking this junction. If you pass the junction, the trail continues for another mile and fades away near Pilgrim Creek.

The trail to the right climbs about 50 feet and enters a stand of mixed conifers, which appears to be good habitat for woodpeckers and owls; it then joins a ravine. The ridge to the right shades its north-facing slope from the sun, keeping the forest floor damp. Thimbleberry, monkey flower, and monkshood grow around small, seasonal ponds. Eventually the ravine opens a bit, allowing the sun to dry out the slope on the left. The conifer forest consequently gives way to an almost treeless meadow.

After .75 mile, the trail comes to a sign. Turn right to climb .9 mile to Grand View Point (see the trail description later in this section). If you are going to Two Ocean Lake, continue straight. The trail leads through the forest for about .5 mile before joining another trail coming from the right. The intersection is marked by a red trail marker, but no sign. The right fork follows the southwest side of the lake to the Two Ocean Lake parking area. Continuing straight, the trail follows the northeast side of the lake to the same parking area. The following description continues along the straight path, assuming a morning start and a preference to hike the sunny (northeast) side of the lake in the morning and the shady (southwest) side later when the sun is hot.

NOTE: If this intersection is reached by coming from the Two Ocean Lake parking area, the hike can be continued around the lake; or the 2.8-mile roundtrip hike up to Grand View Point can be made before finishing the hike around the lake. The Grand View Point description is near the end of this section.

Shortly after the intersection, the trail emerges from the forest and crosses a footbridge at the head of Two Ocean Lake. Often swans and ducks (and occasionally loons and grebes) are found in this bay at the extreme northwest end of the lake. Woodpeckers nest in the aspen stand ahead. On the sunny northeast side of the lake, the trail leads through a variety of vegetation. In summer the birdwatching is good, and so are the opportunities to see wildflowers and butterflies. Large mammals (elk, deer, and moose) may also be seen, especially in morning and evening.

The Tetons offer a spectacular view beyond the opposite shore. About a third of the way along the lake there is a large bay with a beaver lodge on the shore.

Snow melts relatively quickly on the sunny northeast side of the lake, making it a good early season hike. Many little feeder creeks keep the meadows wet and support a multitude of wildflowers. Willows grow near the lake. The lower, wetter meadows tend to be grassy, while sagebrush becomes more prevalent higher on the slopes.

The meadows near the lake are among the loveliest in the valley. Soft, pastel pinks (sticky geraniums) and blues (lupine) are lightly accented with yellows (cinquefoil), reds (paintbrush), and white (asters), creating an unforgettable landscape of natural colors.

Near the east end of the lake the trail enters a small, mixed forest. It arrives at the lake's outlet, which winds through a marsh and empties into Pacific Creek about 2 miles downstream. Gilia and hare-bells flank the path leading down to the stream. Dams attest to the presence of beavers, and a variety of birds is supported by this marshy habitat.

After crossing a footbridge, the trail leads up a hill to the Two Ocean Lake parking area. Two trails leave the far side of the parking area. The one to the left connects with Emma Matilda Lake Trail. The trail to the right follows the southwest shore of Two Ocean Lake.

The continuation of the Two Ocean Lake Trail sets off through a lodgepole pine forest with a blue floor of lupine. Water hemlock, a toxic plant similar to cow parsnip, may be found near the path. Lodgepole pine eventually gives way to a dense, old-growth spruce/fir forest. Very little sunlight filters through the canopy of this woods. The soil is more moist, supporting a different understory.

Two meadows interrupt the forest along the way, both of them full of flowers. The second meadow gracefully flanks a drainage flowing from a small glacial pond above. The trail crosses this drainage, climbs about 100 feet above the lake, then switches back down near the lakeshore. Swainson's thrushes continue their flute-like phrases well into July, even after many other birds have stopped singing.

There is a trail junction 2.4 miles from the Two Ocean Lake parking area. This is the unmarked trail intersection with the trail from the Grand View Point parking area that was pointed out earlier in this description. This junction marks the completion of the loop around Two Ocean Lake. One-half mile to the left is the intersection with the trail to Grand View Point. At the Grand View Point junction, continue straight and retrace the earlier route to the parking area, or turn left and return via Grand View Point.

During the ascent to Grand View Point, the forest changes from lodgepole pine to subalpine fir to Douglas fir as the trail switches back up the hill. Huckleberry and grouse whortleberry may be found along the way. They're good to eat, but remember that bears like them too. While staying alert for bears, also keep an eye open for accipiters. This habitat is ideal for these long-tailed, short-winged hawks of the forest, as well as for owls. Higher up the mountain, tall white, daisy-like Engelmann asters grow along the trail.

There are many wildflowers at the top of the hill but, in the spring, balsamroot clearly dominates the scene. After the snow melts, this showy flower paints the mountaintop a buttery yellow. Spreading dogbane occupies a small area on the southeast face of the mountaintop, sometimes playing host to dozens of fritillary and other butterflies.

Two red outcroppings are rather prominent features near the summit. The rock, andesite, is volcanic. Interestingly, glacial boulders are mixed in with the andesite, revealing that this volcanic activity took place before the Pacific Creek glaciation 70,000 years ago.

The panorama from Grand View Point can be very three-dimensional, especially later in the day when shadows are lengthening. The perspective is from a point high enough to see great distances but not so high that the terrain is flattened. Sometimes, especially in the morning and evening, elk and sandhill cranes may be seen in the meadows below. The Teton Wilderness lies to the northeast. Two Ocean and Emma Matilda lakes lie just below. Mount Leidy is in the east, Sleeping Indian is in the southeast, and the Tetons and Jackson Lake are in the west.

The trail continues down to the Grand View Point parking area, leading through a mixed forest with large Douglas firs. To return to the trailhead, walk down the road that leads up to the parking area then turn right.

CHRISTIAN POND LOOP

The walk around Christian Pond is very appealing and very popular. It's not long, and it's relatively flat. The hike offers excellent bird-watching, very good wildflower meadows, a chance to see moose and deer, and some good views of the Tetons. Trumpeter swans may be seen on Christian Pond, and sometimes they nest there. Many other migratory waterfowl also nest there. This is a very sensitive wildlife area. Please stay on the trail and do not try to approach the pond more closely than the trail permits! You will see much more if you bring binoculars or a spotting scope.

*Trumpeter Swans frequent the Christian Pond-
Two Ocean Lake waters.*

LENGTH: 3.7 miles around Christian Pond.

DIFFICULTY: The hike is rated *easy.* The trail is fairly flat, and the footing is good. Some of the intersections are not well marked. Staying left at each trail junction keeps the hiker on the main trail around the lake.

ELEVATION: The trail has only a few hills, and they vary less than 200 feet from a base altitude of 6,800 feet.

ACCESS: From the Moran Entrance Station to Grand Teton National Park, continue north 4 miles on Highway 89 to Jackson Lake Junction. Bear right at this junction and stay on Highway 89 for .9 mile. Park just north of the bridge in the small parking area on the right.

MAP: Colter Bay and Jackson Lake Lodge Area, page 94.

TRAIL DESCRIPTION: From the parking area, the trail descends a small hill into a willow-filled marsh. Flycatchers, warblers, sparrows, soras, snipe, and sandhill cranes inhabit these lowlands. The trail crosses Christian Creek and, after about .3 mile, climbs the moraine that impounds Christian Pond.

Near the top of the hill is a small overlook of the pond. *Please don't leave this area for a closer look.* Usually trumpeter swans are visible, and this is the best place in the valley to see ruddy ducks. When in breeding plumage, the males have cinnamon bodies, a white cheek patch, an eye-catching powder-blue bill, and a tail that often is held straight up.

Near the pond's south end, scarlet gilia, balsamroot, harebells, lupine, sticky geranium, and buckwheat may all be found along the path.

To continue around Christian Pond, stay left at the trail junction. The trail ascends through mixed woodland stands and small meadows. It enters a conifer forest then emerges from the trees and parallels the forest. There is a large meadow on the left gently leading up to a ridge. The meadow is blanketed with a variety of wildflowers including gilia, balsamroot, daisies, asters, lupine, flax, and harebells. Towhees also inhabit this meadow, and from the ridge is a marvelous view of the Tetons beyond Jackson Lake Lodge.

As you continue your hike, the trail intersects Emma Matilda Trail. To return to the parking area, stay left and descend once again into the willow flats. Moose are frequently seen browsing in this area, so be careful. The trail then climbs the ridge to the west and follows it south to the parking area.

EMMA MATILDA LAKE TRAIL

The south side of Emma Matilda Lake is cloaked with a dense forest of old Engelmann spruce and subalpine fir. A ridge on the north side separates Emma Matilda Lake from nearby Two Ocean Lake and affords dramatic views of the Tetons and Jackson Lake. A 9.7-mile trail encircles Emma Matilda Lake. The trails in the Emma Matilda/Two Ocean Lake area do not receive as much visitation as the trails near Colter Bay, so they provide hikers with plenty of solitude.

Wildlife abounds, including black and grizzly bears, elk, moose, mule deer, ospreys, and bald eagles. Because of the abundance of bears in this area, it is wise to make noise while hiking and to be alert for fresh bear signs.

LENGTH: From the Two Ocean Lake parking area, the hike is 11.7 miles. From Jackson Lake Lodge, the hike is 11 miles.

DIFFICULTY: The hike, rated as *moderate*, is relatively long but mostly level except for two steep sections where the trail ascends and descends the ridge on the north side of the lake.

ELEVATION: Emma Matilda Lake lies at 6,873 feet. The trail reaches about 7,280 feet along the ridge north of the lake, an elevation gain of about 400 feet.

ACCESS: From Jackson Lake Lodge, follow the trail east from the corral, under the highway bridge, to Christian Pond. For access from Two Ocean Lake, park at the Two Ocean Lake parking area and follow the trail leaving the southwest corner of the parking area.

MAP: Colter Bay and Jackson Lake Lodge Area, page 94.

TRAIL DESCRIPTION: The trail to Emma Matilda Lake leaves the Two Ocean Lake parking area and heads up the ridge between the two lakes. Open lodgepole pine forest alternates with meadows of wildflowers along the 1 mile walk to the trail around Emma Matilda Lake. The trail along the northern side of Emma Matilda climbs up a ridge 400 feet above the lake. Open Douglas fir forest and meadows cloak the top of the ridge.

In the summer of 1994, lightning started a fire on top of this ridge. Drought conditions dictated fire suppression, so fire-fighting efforts contained the burn at about 50 acres. The trail crosses through the burned area, allowing hikers to witness the pattern of plant growth after the fire.

The trail descends the western end of the ridge and looks down on Christian Pond and Jackson Lake Lodge. Panoramic views west to the Tetons are spectacular, especially when vegetation turns a lush green in spring and early summer.

A left turn at the trail junction near the base of the ridge leads along a sagebrush-covered ridge to the south side of Emma Matilda Lake, while the trail straight ahead (west) goes to Jackson Lake Lodge via Christian Pond. A short side trip to Lookout Rock provides close-up views of the southwest corner of Emma Matilda Lake. Then the trail plunges into a dense forest of Engelmann spruce and subalpine fir that lines the southern side of the lake. In spring, tiny pink calypso orchids bloom in rotting logs on the moist forest floor.

At the southeast point of kidney-bean shaped Emma Matilda Lake, the trail swings away from the lakeshore through several aspen groves of various ages and sizes. The highlands seen to the northeast are part of the vast Teton Wilderness. The trail continues around the lake to the junction with the spur trail back to the Two Ocean Lake parking area.

SIGNAL MOUNTAIN TRAIL

This hike is quite different from others in the park, and it has quite a lot to offer. It's relatively short and can be done in a few hours. There are fine views of the mountains and it presents a good perspective from which to study the geology of Jackson Hole. There is a diversity of habitats, thus an abundance of birds and other wildlife. Best of all, the trail is not well traveled by hikers since a road goes up Signal Mountain, providing an easier access.

LENGTH: 5.5 miles.

DIFFICULTY: The hike is rated *moderate*. The trail is well marked, and the footing is good.

ELEVATION: The hike begins at 6,960 feet and climbs to Jackson Point Overlook at 7,593 feet, a gain of only 633 feet. The hike may seem more arduous because much of it takes place up and down hills, and there is a fairly steep ascent to Jackson Point that gains 600 feet in less than 1 mile.

ACCESS: From the Moran Entrance Station to Grand Teton National Park, continue north 4 miles on Highway 89 to Jackson Lake Junction. Bear left toward the dam and take Teton Park Road south to the intersection with Signal Mountain Road (4.1 miles). Turn left and drive 1.1 miles. Pull off the road just before the pond on the right. There is an unmarked trail on the near (west) side of the pond.

MAP: Colter Bay and Jackson Lake Lodge Area, page 94.

TRAIL DESCRIPTION: Follow the path along the west shoreline of the pond. Sometimes moose feed in or near the pond. Great gray owls have nested in the area. Lupine, harebells, and paintbrush sprinkle color along the trail winding its way through a lodgepole pine forest.

The trail leaves the pond and comes to a fork with a sign showing two routes to Jackson Point Overlook; essentially, the two routes form a loop. One reason to go right "Via Ponds" and return "Via Ridge" is that the ridge is higher and relatively open and, when returning toward the west, the hike affords great views of the Tetons.

The right fork ("Via Ponds") starts off through a meadow filled with asters, gilia, and balsamroot. Then it enters a mixed stand of aspens and conifers. Blue grouse inhabit the Signal Mountain area; these birds may be seen anywhere along the trail and even in open areas around Jackson Point Overlook. The trail also passes near some ponds on which ducks are often seen.

The climb to the summit begins just before the path is rejoined by the "Via Ridge" trail. This junction is 1 mile from the overlook. Giant hyssop, little sunflowers, geraniums, hawkweed, gilia, and cinquefoil may be found along the path. Aspen stands are interspersed among large Douglas firs.

Jackson Point Overlook is surrounded by wildflowers, so hummingbirds may sometimes be seen buzzing and humming among the plants. A walk around the sagebrush often reveals a grouse running for cover. The real show up here, however, is the geology exhibit that unfolds before your eyes.

The Burned Ridge moraine is actually a series of conifer-covered moraines marking the southernmost advance of the glaciers present in the valley about 15,000 years ago. The vast sageflats to the south of the moraine form the outwash plain of that same glaciation. To the southeast are several glacial kettles or "potholes". Sometimes swans can be seen on these ponds.

The moraine containing Jackson Lake also is clearly visible from the overlook. Near the base of the Teton Range to the southwest, the moraines impounding Phelps, Taggart, Bradley, Jenny, and Leigh lakes may also be seen.

Returning on the same trail, after a mile of downhill walking, the trail forks. The "Via Ridge" trail to the right offers gorgeous views of the Teton Range. This route completes the loop near the pond where you started the hike.

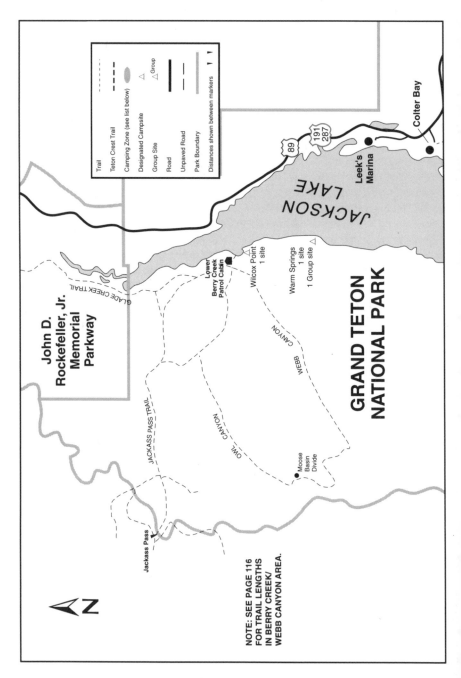

BERRY CREEK/WEBB CANYON AREA MAP

NORTH TETON TRAILS FROM BERRY CREEK/WEBB CANYON AREA

BERRY CREEK—OWL CREEK LOOP
WEBB AND OWL CANYONS.
BERRY CREEK FROM THE CUTOFF TO JACKASS PASS
GLADE CREEK TRAIL

BERRY CREEK/WEBB CANYON AREA TRAILS

Access to these trails and other canyons to the north involves crossing Jackson Lake in a canoe or hiking from the trailhead on the Grassy Lake Road. Canoe crossings should be made when there is little wind; mornings are generally best. Motor shuttles may be arranged (a fee is charged) at the Colter Bay Marina; call (307) 543-2811.

Trails in the Berry Creek/Webb Canyon area receive minimal maintenance, and there are no bridges across the streams. Hiking in all these canyons includes stream crossings that can be difficult at high water. Safe use of these areas requires that all hikers be in good physical condition and experienced with topographic map and compass use. Both black and grizzly bears inhabit the area. Patrols are infrequent, so hikers must be prepared to evacuate themselves in case of problems.

Despite these considerations, this wild country offers a special attraction to some hikers. Relatively few people visit the area, so it affords a measure of solitude. The mountains are much more gentle than the rugged peaks to the south. Wildflowers abound in the meadows. Elk and bighorn sheep summer on ridges, bears and moose browse in the willows, and harlequin ducks nest by streams.

There are many isolated places to camp in the backcountry, enabling the hiker to explore the wilderness at his or her own pace.

One of the designated campsites on the west side of Jackson Lake may be reserved for up to three nights. Using a designated campsite as a base camp enables hikers to explore the backcountry without having to carry a large backpack.

LENGTH (from the Lower Berry Patrol Cabin):
Jackass Pass Trail/Owl Creek Trail Loop–approximately 10 miles
Jackass Pass Trail to Jackass Pass–approximately 10 miles each way.
Owl Canyon Trail to Moose Basin Divide–approximately 14 miles each way.
Webb Canyon Trail to Moose Basin Divide–approximately 11 miles each way.

DIFFICULTY: These hikes are rated *difficult* for several reasons. The trails are designated near pristine and receive only minimal maintenance (stabilization of erosion, rudimentary marking, and minimal clearing of debris); footing is often difficult; the trailhead is relatively inaccessible; and there are no bridges and numerous stream crossings. Carry a pair of stream crossing shoes, such as old sneakers or rubber sandals, with you. Stated mileages on these trails are less precise than those for the park's southern trails. Hikers should carry and know how to use a topographical map and a compass.

ELEVATION: Jackson Lake lies at 6,772 feet, and the Lower Berry Creek patrol cabin is just a few feet higher. The loop trail gains about 800 feet—much of the elevation is gained crossing the ridge between Berry Creek and Owl Creek. Jackass Pass lies at 8,450 feet (about 1,670 feet higher than the patrol cabin). Moose Basin Divide lies at 9,840 feet (about 3,050 feet higher than the patrol cabin).

ACCESS: Take Highway 89 north from Jackson Lake Junction to the Lizard Creek Campground (13 miles). Parking is available for a few cars at the west end of the campground. Canoes may be launched from the beach (a park permit is required). You should not cross unless the lake is smooth and there is no sign of wind.

Lower Berry Creek patrol cabin may also be reached by an 8-mile hike on Glade Creek Trail from Grassy Lake Road. Take Highway 89 north from Jackson Lake Junction to the Grassy Lake Road (20 miles). Drive 4.4 miles west on this road to the trailhead parking lot for the 8-mile hike to Lower Berry Creek patrol cabin.

MAP: Berry Creek/Webb Canyon Area, page 114.

TRAIL DESCRIPTIONS: Moose and Berry creek flow into a bay opposite Lizard Creek Campground. On the north side of the bay a white-topped pole marks a path leading through the willows to the trailhead. The lake level is usually high enough that a wade into the willows is necessary to find a place to tie up your canoe. The showy wildflowers nearby should compensate for any discomfort you experience because of the mud oozing between your toes. Monkshood, paintbrush, tall larkspur, blue flax, bog orchids, and elephanthead grow along the path from the willows to the trailhead. Flycatchers and warblers inhabit the willows. Bears and moose also visit this marshy area.

A very muddy path leads to the Lower Berry patrol cabin. This cabin is literally surrounded by geraniums. Although not required, it's a good idea to register on the sign-in sheet at the trailhead. Three trails head off from here. The one to the south and west leads .1 mile to the trail junction for Owl Creek and Webb Canyon trails. The middle path becomes Jackass Pass Trail (and leads to a junction with the trail to Grassy Lake Road). The path to the right leads north and east—a short walk to an outhouse.

The following trails are maintained at a lesser standard than other trails in the park. These trails are narrow, seldom-traveled footpaths rather than wide, heavily trodden trails. They often can be mistaken for large mammal trails that often join, leave, or cross the trail itself. To stay on the trails, learn to read their signs. For example, at an unmarked, unmapped fork, remember that elk and moose don't bother to clean their trails of debris, so usually the official trail will be the cleaner one. It will also be the one with signs of human activity such as marks of saws and other tools. Also, to encourage hikers to follow a new or modified trail, a log or other hindrance may be placed across the old trail and the new one may be marked with flagging. In any case, at a junction of trails not marked with a metal sign, stop and think about the natural signs. Usually this will serve you well.

BERRY CREEK–OWL CREEK LOOP

Jackass Pass Trail leads through a series of open sagebrush meadows filled with wildflowers and wildlife. Flax, lupine, groundsel, prairie smoke, and geranium present a wonderful display of soft colors. The trail leads up onto a moraine forested with lodgepole pines. Scarlet gilia joins paintbrush and lupine to create a thick, red-and-blue checkerboard carpet. The trail drops to a willow marsh then climbs through a thick lodgepole forest (giving the hiker one last glimpse of

Jackson Lake) after which it bends to the west and drops down to another marsh inhabited by rails and ducks. Cow parsnip and coneflowers grow at the end of the marsh, and pink and white geraniums grow under the spruce and pine trees nearby.

The trail winds through a series of meadows with mixed tree stands interspersed among the open areas. A reading of the landscape will, sooner or later, divulge signs of bears. You may spot a tree with a well-worn scratching area and black or brown hairs stuck to the bark. Like most animals, including humans, bears are creatures of habit. If they find a "scratching post" they prefer to others, they will return repeatedly. Evidence of bear digs—places where the earth has been dug up in search of grubs, other insects, or roots—may also be found.

At about 2 miles the trail forks. The right fork (**Glade Creek Trail** description at the end of this section) continues up the west side of Jackson Lake to Grassy Lake Road. The Jackass Pass Trail forks left (west) and intersects Berry Creek Trail in 2.5 miles. This trail rises gently through meadows filled with amazing numbers of wildflowers. Subalpine firs begin to mix in with spruce and pine in forested areas. At one point, there is a good view of the Snake River with Steamboat Mountain off in the distant east.

As the trail approaches the burn on the hill, another bear sign may be seen: trees completely girdled or stripped of bark. These powerful animals rip the bark off the tree with their claws then rake their front teeth over the cambium for food. This behavior is most prevalent in the early spring when little other food is available and the bears are hungry after a long, inactive winter.

Lazuli buntings may be found in the mixed open stands of trees. Geraniums and lupine paint the meadows a wonderful pastel pink and blue. The burn on the ridge to the right is the lightning-caused Dave Adams Hill Fire of 1987. Soon the trail leads down a gentle drainage too damp for trees but not for bistort, the puffy, small white flowers on long stems.

At about 4 miles, the trail forks. The trail to **Jackass Pass** (see the description later in this section) continues straight. The left fork connects with the Owl Creek Trail in 2 miles and then loops back to the Lower Berry Creek patrol cabin.

Soon after taking the left fork, the trail comes to Berry Creek. Fording this creek is hardly ever easy. Remember to put on your stream-crossing shoes. The best technique is to use a stout pole as a "third leg", crossing the stream moving only one "leg" at a time and always maintaining a firm base.

After crossing Berry Creek, the trail climbs through a dense conifer forest onto a ridge that offers a good view of Owl Peak. The trail then switches back to the left and descends to the junction with Owl Creek Trail, 4 miles from Jackson Lake.

Soon the trail recrosses Berry Creek, requiring another fording just above the stream's confluence with Owl Creek. Owl Canyon is filled with willows, marshes, and beaver ponds. The narrow trail clings to the side of a ridge and affords great views of Berry Creek below. Douglas firs grow on this south facing slope. Taking the time to sit among the wildflowers and search the willows below for a moose or a bear may be rewarding. Sometimes harlequin ducks can be spotted in the creek.

Farther downstream the canyon narrows and the creek moves faster. The trail approaches the edge of the steep canyon wall and sometimes seems to hang over the creek. These overlooks are good places to see harlequin ducks and American dippers. One overlook is perched just downstream from a roaring cascade.

Finally the trail emerges from the canyon and runs through a sagebrush meadow and along Berry Creek. It then joins the Webb Canyon Trail shortly before the Lower Berry Creek patrol cabin.

WEBB AND OWL CANYONS

The trail heads west from the Lower Berry Creek patrol cabin across a sagebrush meadow. On the west side of the dry meadow, a left turn at the trail sign for Webb Canyon leads to a fording of Moose Creek. Early in the season this stream crossing can be formidable—over 3 feet high. Again, use stream crossing shoes that will allow easier walking over rocky stream bottoms and will keep your hiking boots dry. On the south side of Berry Creek, the trail climbs a gentle ridge and hugs the edge of the forest, then continues on the uphill edge of a willow marsh. Beware of numerous elk trails that crisscross the official trail—wildlife trails are not lined with sawed trees, nor are downed trees ever removed from them.

The trail winds west into the canyon below imposing outcropped layers of sedimentary rock on the north side. It then follows along Moose Creek through stands of spruce and fir that alternate with open meadows. For about 2 miles, the trail steadily gains elevation and climbs over metamorphic basement rock along the fast-flowing creek. Then the canyon opens up, and the trail provides a view of the rock walls facing the upper canyon.

After the trail drops down to the creek, it goes through boulder fields and eventually follows a calmer, willow-lined section of the creek below sheer rock walls. After traversing rolling terrain, the trail

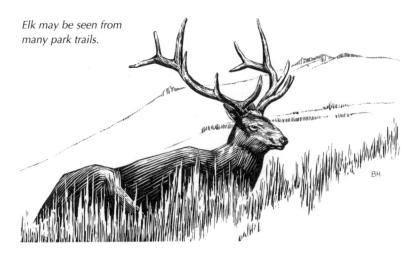

Elk may be seen from many park trails.

BH

climbs steadily up open meadows of wildflowers and grasses growing on limestone. Above are twin peaks of sedimentary rock: Owl Peak to the east and Elk Mountain to the west.

An older trail used to cross the creek in this area, but a reroute in the mid-1980s eliminated this stream ford. The new trail follows an old forest service trail and switches back up to avoid an outcropping of crumbly rock. The trail continues up and across wildflower-filled slopes to a waterfall where spring-fed water tumbles over a limestone wall.

After the falls, the trail switches back up the north side of the canyon over loose talus that supports numerous wildflowers, then enters Moose Basin, a magnificent open bowl. Islands of Engelmann spruce and subalpine fir dot these expansive high-elevation meadows. From Moose Basin to Moose Basin Divide, the steep trail is marked with rock cairns. Moose Basin Divide, at 9,840, feet separates the Moose Creek and the Berry Creek/Owl Creek drainages. At the divide, massive Mount Moran dominates the view south, with Doane Peak in the southeast, at the head of Waterfalls Canyon. The view north includes the Red Mountains and Pitchstone Plateau of Yellowstone National Park.

From the divide, the trail descends over loose limestone talus into a cirque at the head of Owl Canyon. Krummholz (stunted) vegetation clings to the uppermost ridgetops. Lower down in the cirque, the ridges host islands of taller spruce and fir. The trail continues to drop into Owl Canyon over soft mounds of shale that are laced with springs. Bluebells, cow parsnip, western coneflower, and other tall wildflowers carpet these upper meadows.

The trail next leads down into the V-shaped western end of Owl

Canyon through extensive stands of mature spruce and fir that provide welcome shade on hot summer days. Occasional openings in the forest support meadow vegetation.

About 6 miles from Moose Basin Divide, the trail crosses to the south side and follows gently meandering Owl Creek. This stretch of canyon is wide and U-shaped with a flat bottom. The trail is easy to lose when it crosses back to the north side after about 1 mile.

The trail now skirts the edge of a large willow meadow and a freshwater marsh where beaver signs, such as dams and lodges, are plentiful. At the junction, the trail joins the cutoff trail and fords Berry Creek. Except in spring and early summer, this stream crossing is one of the easier ones in this part of the park.

BERRY CREEK FROM THE CUTOFF TO JACKASS PASS

About 1 mile west of the Berry Creek cutoff, the trail to Upper Berry Creek leaves the conifer forest and enters an extensive willow marsh. The trail parallels the north side of the creek then enters a mature lodgepole pine forest, avoiding the marsh that fills the wide, flat bottom of Berry Canyon. Beaver, moose, and elk find suitable habitat in this marsh. Hechtman Horse Camp lies about 100 yards west of where Hechtman Creek enters the upper meadows. The creek has no bridge, and even in late summer the rock hopping isn't easy; early in the summer, the ford may be very difficult. Hikers anticipating panoramic views will be rewarded after leaving the forest.

Shortly after passing the Upper Berry Creek patrol cabin (on the south side of the creek), the trail begins a relatively gentle ascent toward Jackass Pass. The last half mile before the pass is steep with four or five switchbacks on the north side of the bowl. Here the trail is almost completely in the open. At the top of the switchbacks, the trail circles the rim of the bowl to the southwest and affords good views of the bowl, the west side of Forellen Peak, and the upper reaches of Elk Mountain.

GLADE CREEK TRAIL

Glade Creek Trail provides access to trails in the northwestern corner of Grand Teton National Park without crossing Jackson Lake. From the Glade Creek Trailhead to the Lower Berry Creek patrol cabin is 8 miles. The trail is relatively level, losing little more than 100 feet in elevation from Grassy Lake Road to the patrol cabin.

From the trailhead, the trail leads south through an open lodgepole pine forest, then descends to cross Glade Creek via a footbridge. The trail soon leaves the conifer forest to traverse moist meadows lining the Snake River. During mosquito season, this section of trail can be oppressive, although it is always scenic. Where the Snake River enters Jackson Lake, the trail leaves the riparian meadows and passes through forests of tall subalpine fir and Engelmann spruce. It then climbs a ridge and enters a willow meadow. The junction with the trail going west to Jackass Pass is in this willow meadow.

The trail to the Lower Berry Creek patrol cabin continues south and has been described above.

Part III
FLORA AND FAUNA

arrowleaf balsamroot

WILDFLOWERS, SHRUBS & TREES

During late spring and summer, colorful wildflowers provide breathtaking displays in various parts of the park. Blooming follows snowmelt, so the show moves upslope as the season progresses.

June in Jackson Hole brings flowers in the valley. Clumps of yellow arrowleaf balsamroot, a daisy-like flower with arrow-shaped leaves, add vivid splashes of color to the extensive sagebrush flats. Spikes of blue-purple lupines, a member of the pea family, flower along streams in the southern half of Jackson Hole. Later in the summer, other species of lupine, also blue-purple, bloom in open conifer forests.

The meadows in the valley reach peak flowering during July. Look for yellow mountain sunflowers, pink mountain hollyhock, purple lupines, pink sticky geraniums, scarlet gilia, and purple upland larkspur.

As snow melts in the canyons between Teton peaks, hikers are treated to meadows with an exquisite mix of colors: white columbine, bluebells, red paintbrush, pink daisies, and lavender asters. Along canyon streams the vegetation is lush, including deep purple monkshood and cow parsnip, with its immense, flat-topped white flower clusters. Canyons with especially magnificent wildflower displays include Open, Cascade, and aptly named Paintbrush.

In alpine areas, above tree line, flowers are diminutive but well worth stooping for. Because of wind, cold temperatures, and the short growing season, alpine flowers tend to grow in ground-hugging cushions. Look for blue alpine forget-me-not, the official flower of Grand Teton National Park, and pink moss campion. Alpine plants are well adapted to their environment, but they are extremely vulnerable to human disturbance. Be sure to stay on established trails.

Parts of the park that have burned in recent years offer a spectacular display of wildflowers because of increased sunlight reaching the forest floor and the fertilizer effect of nitrogen-rich ash. At the Taggart Lake burn area, look for magenta fireweed and yellow heartleaf arnica. Flowering shrubs that have proliferated since the fire include pink spreading dogbane and snowbrush ceanothus with its sweet-scented blossoms. Wildflowers bloom amid stands of shoulder-high aspens and numerous lodgepole pines that grew after the fire, so hiking the Taggart Lake Trail provides a close-up view of accelerated plant growth as a result of fire.

Two good reference books for Jackson Hole wildflowers are *Plants of Yellowstone and Grand Teton National Parks* by Richard J. Shaw and *Rocky Mountain Wildflowers* by John J. and Frank C. Craighead, and Ray J. Davis (see **Recommended Books**).

Enjoy the wildflowers, but please leave them for others to appreciate. Picking wildflowers is prohibited within Grand Teton National Park. However, edible berries, plants, and mushrooms may be gathered by hand for personal daily consumption. Be certain of plant identification before eating parts of any wild plants.

FLOWERING SEASONS OF SELECTED FLOWERS AND SHRUBS

FLOWERS	VALLEY	CANYONS	ALPINE
WHITE			
Mountain Ash		Jul	
Birchleaf Spirea	Jul	Jul	
Woodlandstar	Jun		
Richardson Geranium	Jun-Aug	Jun-Aug	
Thimbleberry		Jun-Jul	
Green Gentian	Jun-Jul	Jul-mid Aug	
Cowparsnip	late Jun-mid Aug		
Ladies-tresses	Aug-mid Sep	Aug-Sep	
Rocky Mountain Parnassus	Jul	Aug	Aug
Parrots-Beak *(leafy lousewort)*	Jul	Aug	
Pussy Toes *(several species)*	Jun-Aug	Jul-Aug	Jul-Aug
Brook Saxifrage		Jul-Aug	
False Solomon Seal	Jun		
Tofieldia		Jun-Aug	
Grouse Whortleberry	Jun	Jun-Jul	
White Bog-Orchid	late Jun-mid Aug	Jul-Aug	
Colorado Columbine		late Jun-Aug	
Marsh Marigold		Jun-mid Jul	Jun-Jul
Yampah	Jul-mid Aug	mid Jul-Aug	
Englemann Aster		Jul-Aug	
Yarrow	Jul-early Aug	mid Jul-late Aug	Aug
YELLOW			
Mules-ear Wyethia	mid Jun-Jul		
Hymenoxys			Jul-Aug
Sunflower	mid Jul-Aug		

FLOWERS	VALLEY	CANYONS	ALPINE
YELLOW, CONT.			
Balsamroot	Jun-mid Jul		
Buffaloberry	May-Jun		
Western Coneflower	Aug-Sep	Aug-Sep	
Ivesia	Jun		Aug
Big Sagebrush	Aug-Sep		
Rabbitbrush	mid Aug-Sep		
Heartleaf Arnica	mid Jun-mid Jul	late Jun-late Jul	
Yellow Monkeyflower	Jun-mid Jul	mid Jun-mid Aug	
Subalpine Buttercup		Jul-Aug	
Deathcamas	Jun	mid Jun-early Aug	mid Jul-Aug
Sulfur Buckwheat	mid Jun-mid Aug		
Bracted Lousewort	late Jun-mid Jul	Jul	
Yellow Columbine	late Jun-Jul	Jul-late Aug	
Yellow Fritillary	mid May-mid Jun		
PINK-RED			
Springbeauty	May	Jun-mid Jul	
Sticky Geranium	Jun-Aug		
Globemallow	Jul-mid Aug	mid Jul-Aug	
Steershead	late May-mid Jun	late Jun-mid Jul	
Subalpine Spirea		mid Jul-Aug	
Shooting Star	Jun	late Jun-late Aug	
Ladysthumb Knotweed	Aug		
Lewis Monkeyflower		late Jun-Aug	
Spreading Dogbane	Jul-Aug		
Fireweed	mid Jul-Aug		
Moss Campion			Jul-mid Aug
Calypso Orchid	Jun		
Elephanthead	late Jun-Jul	mid Jul-Aug	
Parry Lousewort			Jul-Aug
Indian Paintbrush	Jun-Jul	Jul-Aug	Jul-early Sep
Skyrocket Gilia	mid Jun-Jul		
BLUE-PURPLE			
Giant Hyssop	Jun-Aug		
Leopard Lily	Jun		
Penstemon *(several species)*	Jun-Jul	Jul-Aug	
Mountain Townsendia			Jul-Aug
Wild Blue Flax	Jul-Aug		
Sky Pilot			Jul-Aug
Monkshood	late Jun-mid Jul	mid Jul-mid Aug	
Low Larkspur	mid May-Jun		
Mountain Bluebell		mid Jul-early Sep	
Fringed Gentian	late Jul-mid Aug	Aug-early Sep	
Harebell	mid Jun-early Sep		
Lupine	Jun-Jul		
Mountain Bog Gentian		late Jul-early Sep	
Silky Phacelia	late Jun-Jul	mid Jul-late Aug	Jul-early Sep
Alpine Forget-me-not			Jul-early Aug

COMMON SHRUBS

ANTELOPE BITTERBRUSH occurs with sagebrush in the southern half of Jackson Hole. Bitterbrush grows up to 3 feet tall. Cream colored flowers bloom in June.

BIG SAGEBRUSH thrives in dry habitats and carpets most of the valley floor. Plants are 1 to 5 feet tall; leaves are grayish-green. Tiny yellow flowers bloom in August.

CHOKECHERRY is a large shrub that grows to 20 feet tall. Cylindrical clusters of showy white flowers bloom in spring.

HUCKLEBERRY grows 2 to 4 feet tall in lodgepole pine forests in the valley and mountain canyons. Tiny purple berries are ripe in August.

MOUNTAIN ASH grows on the lower slopes of the Tetons. This tall shrub has compound leaves. Flat-topped clusters of white flowers bloom in June. In fall, bright orange fruits complement vivid red leaves.

SERVICEBERRY grows to 10 feet tall. Showy white flowers bloom in spring, producing purple berries by late summer.

SNOWBRUSH CEANOTHUS thrives in burned areas. Shiny, leathery green leaves are retained through winter. Clusters of aromatic white flowers bloom in June.

UTAH HONEYSUCKLE grows in open lodgepole pine forests. Leaves are opposite. Cream-colored flowers bloom in early June, producing pairs of fused red, unpalatable berries.

WILLOWS occur in moist areas, especially along stream banks. Twenty species of willow shrubs are found in the park, all having a shrubby growth form. No species of willow trees occur in the park.

TREES

Because of the short growing season, most of the trees in the park are conifers. Conifers retain their leaves (needles) throughout the year and produce food (photosynthesize) on warm spring days. Deciduous trees shed their leaves in the fall, and most of them must grow new leaves in the spring before they can photosynthesize. Exceptions are aspens and cottonwoods, which have chlorophyll in the bark and so are able to photosynthesize before producing leaves.

There are many species of shrubs (including more than twenty in the willow family) in Grand Teton National Park, but the number of trees is not great. The nine described below represent almost all of the area's trees.

BLUE SPRUCE *(Picea pungens)* Fairly common along the Snake River, the blue spruce is hard to find elsewhere. The sharp needles grow singly, have stalks, and are square in cross section. The papery cones are twice as large as those of the Engelmann spruce. With its blue tint and full, graceful profile, the blue spruce is a most attractive conifer.

COTTONWOOD *(Populus angustifolia, Populus acuminata)* This tree can be found throughout the valley in riparian areas. The narrowleaf cottonwood *(Populus angustifolia)* and its various hybrids *(Populus acuminata)* are, aside from the aspen, the most common large, deciduous tree. The bark is a yellow-green color on the young trees and becomes grayish and deeply furrowed on older trees. Mature trees may be 50 to 60 feet high and over 1 foot in diameter. The large, bulky profile is unique among deciduous trees in the park.

DOUGLAS FIR *(Pseudotsuga menziesii)* The "Doug fir" is not a true fir. Its cones fall off and litter the forest floor, offering the best clue to the identity of this species. The papery cones have prickly, trident-shaped bracts growing among the cone scales, and the cones hang down on the tree. Forests of these trees grow on moist, north-facing slopes. The largest specimens, however, grow on drier south-facing slopes, suggesting these slopes once were much damper.

The needles of Douglas firs are thinner near the base. As trees become older, they develop deeply furrowed bark. Their profile is full and not in the typical "Christmas tree" shape.

ENGELMANN SPRUCE *(Picea engelmannii)* The prickly needles of this species grow singly, are square in cross section, and have stalks, leaving its dead twigs rough to the touch. The cones are small (1 to 1.5 inches), papery, and hang below the upper branches. These trees usually grow above 7,000 feet in cool, moist canyons and ravines. The Engelmann's profile is tall, slender, and graceful.

LIMBER PINE (Pinus flexilis) One of two white pines found here, the limber grows below 8,000 feet, often on ridges, and often singly or with just a few other trees. Needles grow in clusters of five. Its green cones are 4 to 5 inches long and substantially larger than those of the whitebark pine. The very flexible branches of the limber permit it to grow in an environment with strong winds. Its irregularly shaped profile is often determined by the prevailing winds.

LODGEPOLE PINE (Pinus contorta) The park's most common conifer, this yellow pine's needles are 2 to 3 inches long and grow in clusters of two. Cones are hard and woody and not soft and papery like the cones of Engelmann spruce and Douglas fir. Lodgepole cones grow on the branches and have sharp pins on their scales. The profile of the lodgepole tends to be tall and slender, especially when growing in dense stands. Branches are confined to the upper parts of the tree; much of the trunk is bare of branches.

QUAKING ASPEN (Populus tremuloides) This deciduous tree is hard to miss in the park. It usually grows in stands that continue to reproduce themselves with shoots growing up from the root system. The smooth, creamy or whitish bark and the light green, rustling or "quaking" leaves identify this tree. Aspens are often mistaken for birch trees, but the only birches found in the park are low shrubs. The profile has a long trunk with a bushy top.

SUBALPINE FIR (Abies lasiocarpa) Grab a branch—if there is no prickliness, it's a fir. This tree grows at elevations up to tree line (10,000 feet), often in mixed stands with lodgepole pine and Engelmann spruce.

Fir needles have no "stalks" at their base. The dead branches are smooth to the touch, having only scars rather than stalks remaining from the needles that have fallen off.

Subalpine firs and other true firs do not drop their cones. Instead, the cones disintegrate and are borne away by the air. Unique among conifers, their cones grow erect from the branches.

The bark is smooth. The profile usually has a long, slender, spire-like top.

WHITEBARK PINE (Pinus albicaulis) Two primary distinctions separate this white pine from the limber pine: The whitebark usually grows above 8,000 feet, and its cones are purple and smaller (2 to 3 inches long). The needles of this white pine species grow in clusters of five. Like the limber pine, the whitebark's branches are very flexible, permitting it to grow in the windy environment near tree line. Its irregular profile also tends to be shaped by the winds.

Priscilla Marsden

Bull Moose

MAMMALS

Grand Teton National Park offers mammals a variety of habitats. Each habitat must supply the basic needs of wildlife: food, water, and cover.

Many small and medium-sized mammals thrive in the park. Some of the most commonly seen include pikas, snowshoe hares, chipmunks, yellow-bellied marmots, red squirrels, muskrats, porcupines, beavers, martens, and weasels.

Frequently seen near trails, larger mammals include coyotes, elk, mule deer, moose, pronghorns, and bison. Bears are occasionally seen. Bighorn sheep sometimes are seen in the high Tetons.

Remember to respect these large creatures! Keep a safe distance to avoid disturbing their routines, and give them their way. Don't run or make abrupt moves or loud noises. Use a telephoto lens to photograph wildlife from a safe distance. Don't try to get closer for that perfect photo.

NOTE: Feeding any wildlife is illegal. Natural food assures their health and survival; staying a safe distance assures yours. Large animals are quick and powerful. Females actively defend their young and predators defend their kills. Approaching too closely may result in serious injury.

IDENTIFYING MAMMALS

BLACK AND GRIZZLY BEARS—Grand Teton National Park provides habitat for black and grizzly bears. Grizzlies have been seen more frequently in recent years, especially in the John D. Rockefeller Parkway and the north end of the Teton Range. Black bears may be found in most parts of the park. They frequent meadows and the lower parts of canyons and are seldom far from the protective cover of trees. Black bears den from fall until spring. Mating occurs in spring and early summer; cubs are born in the winter den. Natural foods include roots, berries, small rodents, and carrion. To distinguish between the two bear species, look for these characteristics.

	BLACK BEAR	GRIZZLY BEAR
Size and weight	Adults are 2.5 to 3 feet at the shoulder and weigh 200 to 300 pounds.	Adults are about 3.5 feet at the shoulder and weigh 300 to 700 pounds.
Color	Varies from black to blond. Many black bears are black with a light brown muzzle.	Varies from black to blond. Dark fur with long, pale guard hairs accounts for a dark and light, or grizzled, appearance.
Appearance	Straight face; no shoulder hump; rump higher than shoulders.	Dished-in face; tiny ears; prominent shoulder hump; rump lower than shoulders.
Claws	Short and curved for climbing. Claws do not always show in tracks.	Long and straight. Claws often show in tracks.

Bull moose (foreground), bull elk and buck deer have antlers that are shed in winter or early spring. New antlers grow each spring and summer. Females do not grow antlers.

Mule deer

Named for their large, mule-like ears, mule deer have a brown body, white rump patch, and white tail tipped with black. Only males have antlers. Made of bone, antlers grow throughout the summer, then are shed each winter. One or two spotted fawns are born in June. Mule deer browse on woody plants, and they frequent open forests and meadow edges at dusk and dawn.

Elk (WAPITI)

Nearly 95,000 elk live in the Greater Yellowstone Ecosystem. This large member of the deer family has a dark brown head, neck and legs; light brown body; and pale rump patch. Large antlers distinguish mature, healthy bulls. Most visible during spring and fall, elk migrate between high summer meadows and lower winter range. During rut (the breeding season that occurs each fall) bull elk will bugle and defend harems of cows. Spotted calves are born in the spring during migration to the high country. Elk prefer ecotones (edges) between forests and meadows. Grazers, they rest in forests by day and feed on meadow grasses at night.

Moose

Largest member of the deer family, moose have dark brown bodies with long, light colored legs; humped shoulders; and a dewlap hanging from their necks. Bulls have large palmate antlers. After fall breeding, one or two rusty-brown calves are born in May or June. Primarily browsers, they rely heavily on willows and can be found year-round in willow thickets. In summer they also feed on more succulent vegetation in ponds and streams.

Pronghorn (Antelope)

Two white neck bands distinguish pronghorn, the fastest mammal in North America. Both males and females have horns, but the male's horns are larger. Pronghorn permanently retain their horns but annually shed the sheaths covering them. Pronghorn breed in September; young are born in the spring. These small ungulates (hooved animals) frequent the sagebrush flats where they feed on sagebrush and grasses.

Bison (Buffalo)

A massive head, a shoulder hump, and a large dark brown body identify the bison. Both cows and bulls have curved horns that continue to grow throughout life. Bulls weigh up to 2,000 pounds. Bison breed in late summer and early fall. Females usually produce one calf in the spring. Found in meadows, sagebrush flats, and open forests, bison feed on grasses and sedges. Despite their placid appearance, bison have seriously injured people who approach too closely.

Yellow-bellied Marmot

Brown with a bushy tail and yellowish belly, this chunky rodent weighs 5 to 10 pounds. A melanistic (black) form also occurs in Grand Teton. Marmots feed entirely on vegetation and live in dens, often in rocky places. During winter, marmots hibernate. Look for marmots in canyons and listen for their loud alarm whistle.

Golden-mantled Ground Squirrel

Often mistaken for a chipmunk, this ground squirrel has a coppery head, no face stripes, and white side stripes with black borders. Frequently seen on mountain trails, golden-mantled ground squirrels live on brushy talus slopes. Constantly active in summer, they hibernate in winter.

Uinta Ground Squirrel

The most frequently seen mammal in the park in the summer, the Uinta ground squirrel has a grayish body and short tail. Abundant in sagebrush and near human settlements, they feed on plants and scavenge on carrion. This relative of the prairie dog lives in burrows, where it hibernates from August to April. When alarmed, Uinta ground squirrels stand on their hind legs and whistle before diving into their burrows. When you hear local people talk about "chiselers", they are usually referring to Uinta ground squirrels.

RED SQUIRREL
Chestnut upper parts, white below, with a dark stripe between. This tree squirrel has a buffy eye ring and a bushy tail; inhabits conifers. Scolding territorial call, heard all year by hikers walking through forest, is a loud, fast rattle several seconds long. About 12-15 inches in length.

PIKA
Closely related to rabbits, pikas have small round ears and no tail. Pikas inhabit alpine and subalpine talus slopes where they feed on grasses and other plants. During the winter, pikas do not hibernate; they remain active, feeding on vegetation they dried in "haystacks" in late summer. Pikas are often seen in mountain canyons—listen for their distinctive "bleating" call.

SNOWSHOE HARE
Large hare, about 15-20 inches in length. Inhabits coniferous forests with dense undergrowth. Large ears and hind feet (hence, its name). In winter, this animal is white with black-tipped ears; in summer, it is gray/brown with black-tipped ears and light tail. This nocturnal hare is not often seen. Populations are very cyclic.

LEAST CHIPMUNK

The two chipmunks commonly seen in the park are difficult to tell apart. The least chipmunk averages about 10% smaller in size than the yellow-pine chipmunk. Look for alternating dark and light stripes on back and sides of animal. Quick, darting behavior with tail held straight up distinguishes this chipmunk. Prefers sagebrush and other dry habitat.

YELLOW-PINE CHIPMUNK
Similar to least chipmunk but slightly larger. Commonly seen in forest openings. Coloration and markings very similar to least chipmunk, but movement is more deliberate and less jerky.

BEAVER
This large aquatic rodent has a dark brown body and a flat, paddle-shaped tail. Primarily nocturnal, beavers prefer to feed on willows and aspen. Beavers dam streams to form ponds; they also build lodges of branches and saplings held together with mud. River-dwelling beavers burrow into banks.

MUSKRAT

This animal is much smaller than a beaver, less than half its length and only 5-10% of its weight. Their habitat is similar; muskrat often may be found in beaver ponds and slow-moving streams. This dark brown animal has a long, rudder-like tail, a large head and small ears and eyes.

PORCUPINE

These slow-moving, rather large (about 3-4 feet long and weighing 10-40 pounds) rodents have quills on their backs from head to tail. While they prefer being close to water, they may be found in almost any habitat. Porcupines eat the inner bark of pine trees, often girdling and seriously damaging them.

RIVER OTTER

Found in or near rivers, ponds, and lakes, this large member of the weasel family has webbed feet, a brown streamlined body, and a thick tail that gradually tapers toward the tip. River otters feed mostly on fish. For dens, river otters burrow into the banks of streams or use old beaver lodges.

MARTEN

Arboreal (tree-climbing) members of the weasel family, martens inhabit coniferous forests. Martens weigh 1 to 3 pounds and have a brown body with an orange throat patch. Martens prey on squirrels, mice, and birds and scavenge on carrion.

COYOTE

Much smaller than a gray wolf, this member of the dog family usually weighs about 25 to 35 pounds (a gray wolf may weigh over 100 pounds). Because coyotes in this area are larger than average, they are frequently mistaken for wolves. Coyotes breed in winter, with a litter of four to six pups born in the spring. Coyotes prey on rodents and scavenge on carrion. Their varied habitat includes sagebrush flats, river bottoms, and grassy meadows. Listen for their howling at dawn, dusk, and throughout the night.

LONG-TAILED WEASEL

About 1-1.5 feet in length, this animal is active day and night, and is seen by hikers with some frequency in a variety of habitats. It has a long body and tail, short legs, and a pointed face. In winter, the animal is white with a black tip on its tail. In summer, it is brown with light underparts and feet and a black-tipped tail.

LITTLE BROWN BAT

These most misunderstood mammals are unique: their wings are modified hands; they hunt insects at night using echolocation, which is similar to sonar; and they catch and consume up to 2,000 mosquitoes a night. Breeding occurs in late fall, with one young born in the spring. Little brown bats frequently roost in buildings or under the bark of trees.

MAMMAL CHECKLIST

Key To Symbols

a ABUNDANT – frequently seen in appropriate habitat and season.

c COMMON – seen occasionally in appropriate habitat and season.

u UNCOMMON – seen irregularly in appropriate habitat and season.

r RARE – seldom seen even in appropriate habitat and season.

x ACCIDENTAL or SURPRISING – out of known range.

? QUESTIONABLE – verification unavailable

INSECTIVORA - Insect-eaters

☐ c - Masked Shrew
☐ c - Vagrant Shrew
☐ r - Dwarf Shrew
☐ u - Northern Shrew

CHIROPTERA - Bats

☐ c - Little Brown Bat
☐ u - Long-eared Myotis
☐ u - Long-legged Myotis
☐ u - Silver-haired Myotis
☐ r - Hoary Bat
☐ u - Big Brown Bat

LAGOMORPHA - Rabbits and Hares

☐ c - Pika
☐ c - Snowshoe Hare
☐ u - White-tailed Jackrabbit

RODENTIA - Gnawing Mammals

☐ c - Least Chipmunk
☐ c - Yellow Pine Chipmunk
☐ a - Mountane Vole
☐ a - Beaver
☐ a - Deer Mouse
☐ u - Bushy-tailed Woodrat
☐ c - Southern Red-backed Vole
☐ c - Heather Vole
☐ u - Northern Flying Squirrel
☐ u - Uinta Chipmunk
☐ u - Long-tailed Vole
☐ c - Richardson Vole
☐ r - Sagebrush Vole
☐ c - Muskrat
☐ c - Western Jumping Mouse
☐ c - Porcupine
☐ a - Meadows Vole
☐ a - Northern Pocket Gopher
☐ c - Yellow-bellied Marmot
☐ a - Uinta Ground Squirrel
☐ c - Golden-mantled Ground Squirrel
☐ a - Red Squirrel

CARNIVORA - Flesh-eaters

Canidae - Dog Family
- ☐ c - Coyote
- ☐ ? - Gray Wolf
- ☐ r - Red Fox

Ursidae - Bear Family
- ☐ u - Black Bear
- ☐ r - Grizzly Bear

Mustelidae - Weasel Family
- ☐ c - Marten
- ☐ u - Short-tailed Weasel
- ☐ r - Least Weasel
- ☐ c - Long-tailed Weasel
- ☐ u - Mink
- ☐ r - Wolverine
- ☐ c - Badger
- ☐ u - Striped Skunk
- ☐ u - River Otter

Felidae - Cat Family
- ☐ r - Mountain Lion
- ☐ r - Lynx
- ☐ r - Bobcat

Procyonidae - Raccoon Family
- ☐ x - Raccoon

ARTIODACTYLA - Even-toed Hooves

Cervidae - Deer Family
- ☐ a - Wapiti (Elk)
- ☐ c - Mule Deer
- ☐ x - White-tailed Deer
- ☐ a - Moose

Bovidae - Cattle Family
- ☐ c - Bison
- ☐ x - Mountain Goat
- ☐ u - Bighorn Sheep

Antilocapridae - Pronghorn Family
- ☐ c - Pronghorn

Bald eagle and its nest.

BIRDS

Grand Teton National Park encompasses a range of habitats, from alpine meadows to sagebrush flats, from lodgepole pine forests to mountain streams. Birds use habitats that meet their needs for food, water, shelter and nest sites. Some birds frequent only one habitat type while others occupy a variety of habitats. Most of the birds found in the park are migratory, spending only 3-6 months here each year.

There are two good reference books for local birds. *Finding the Birds of Jackson Hole* by Bert Raynes and Darwin Wile is a bird finding guide and includes hikes, maps, habitat descriptions, birding hot spots and a checklist of local birds. *The Birds of Grand Teton National Park* by Bert Raynes includes color photographs and descriptions of many local birds, habitat descriptions and a checklist. Both books are available at the Moose, Colter Bay and Jenny Lake visitor centers.

Enjoy the birds, but be a responsible birder. Nesting birds of all species are easily disturbed. If an adult on a nest flies off at your approach or circles you or screams in alarm, you are too close to the nest. Unattended nestlings readily succumb to predation or exposure to heat, cold and wet weather.

Please report at a visitor center any sightings of birds listed as rare or accidental on the bird checklists.

HOW TO USE THE CHECKLIST OF JACKSON HOLE BIRDS

RELATIVE FREQUENCY OF OCCURRENCE

a ABUNDANT–likely to be seen in large numbers in appropriate habitat and season.

c COMMON–may be observed most of the time and in good numbers in appropriate habitat and season.

o OCCASIONAL–occurs irregularly or in small numbers, but in appropriate habitat and season.

r RARE–unexpected as to season or range.

x ACCIDENTAL or SURPRISING–out of its range, or recorded only once or twice.

? VERIFICATION UNAVAILABLE–additional information especially welcome!

SEASONS

SP March-May   **F September-November**
SU June-August   **W December-February**

BREEDING STATUS
* following species' name indicates nest or dependent young have been observed
• following species' name indicates only circumstantial evidence of breeding.

NO. SPECIES	SP	SU	F	W

LOONS
☐ Red-throated Loon ... x
☐ Pacific Loon ... x ... x
☐ Common Loon* ... o ... o ... o ... x

GREBES
☐ Pied-billed Grebe* ... o ... o ... o ... r
☐ Horned Grebe ... r ... r ... o
☐ Red-necked Grebe ... x ... x
☐ Eared Grebe• ... c ... o ... o
☐ Western Grebe* ... o ... o ... c
☐ Clark's Grebe ... o ... o ... o

PELICANS
☐ American White Pelican ... c ... c ... c

CORMORANTS
☐ Double-crested Cormorant* ....c...........c ....c..............

BITTERNS AND HERONS
☐ American Bittern* ....o...........o...........o ....
☐ Great Blue Heron* ....c...........c ....c ....o
☐ Great Egret..x...........x ....
☐ Snowy Egret ....r...........r............r ....
☐ Little Blue Heron...............................? ....
☐ Cattle Egret.......................................r ....
☐ Green-backed Heron ....x ....
☐ Black-crowned Night-Heron ....r......................r.............

IBISES
☐ White-faced Ibis ....o ....

WATERFOWL
☐ Tundra Swan......................................o ....o ....o
☐ Trumpeter Swan*...............................c...........c ....c...........c
☐ Greater White-fronted Goose ....x.............
☐ Snow Goose ....o ....o ....r
☐ Ross's Goose x
☐ Canada Goose*..................................c...........c ....c...........c
☐ Wood Duck..r ....r............r...........r
☐ Green-winged Teal* ....c...........c ....c ....o
☐ Mallard*...a...........c ....a..........c
☐ Northern Pintail*...............................o...........o ....o ....o
☐ Blue-winged Teal ....c...........o ....c ....r
☐ Cinnamon Teal* ....c...........c ....o...........x
☐ Northern Shoveler ....o...........o ....o ....o
☐ Gadwall*..c...........c ....c ....o
☐ Eurasian Wigeon ....x...........x ....
☐ American Wigeon*.............................c...........c ....c ....r
☐ Canvasback* ....o...........r ....o ....
☐ Redhead•..o...........o ....c.............
☐ Ring-necked Duck*.............................c...........c ....c ....r
☐ Greater Scaup ....x......................
☐ Lesser Scaup*....................................o...........o ....o ....
☐ Harlequin Duck*................................o...........o ....o ....
☐ Surf Scoter ....x.............
☐ White-winged Scoter...x.............
☐ Common Goldeneye* ....o...........o ....o ....o
☐ Barrow's Goldeneye* ....c...........c ....c ....o
☐ Bufflehead* ....c...........o ....c ....o
☐ Hooded Merganser ....o......................r...........o
☐ Common Merganser* ....c...........c ....c..........c
☐ Red-breasted Merganser ....r......................r ....?

☐ Ruddy Duck* ....o............o ....o............x

VULTURES, HAWKS AND FALCONS
☐ Turkey Vulture ....r ....r.............r...............
☐ Osprey* ....c............c ....c.............
☐ Black-shouldered Kite...x...............
☐ Bald Eagle* ....c............c ....c............c
☐ Northern Harrier ....o............o ....o ....r
☐ Sharp-shinned Hawk* ....o............o ....o............x
☐ Cooper's Hawk* ....o............o ....o............x
☐ Northern Goshawk* ....c............c ....c............o
☐ Broad-winged Hawk.................................x ....?.............
☐ Swainson's Hawk* ....c............c ....c ....
☐ Red-tailed Hawk* ....c............c ....c ....r
☐ Ferruginous Hawk* ....r ....r.............r...............
☐ Rough-legged Hawk ....o....................c ....o
☐ Golden Eagle* ....o............o ....o ....o
☐ American Kestrel* ....c............c ....c ....r
☐ Merlin• ....o ....r ....o............x
☐ Peregrine Falcon* ....r ....r.............r...............r
☐ Gyrfalcon...x ....x............x
☐ Prairie Falcon* ....o............o ....o............x

GALLINACEOUS BIRDS
☐ Gray Partridge* ....r ....r.............r............r
☐ Chukar* ....r ....r.............r............r
☐ Blue Grouse* ....c............c ....c............c
☐ Ruffed Grouse* ....c............c ....c............c
☐ Sage Grouse* ....c............c ....c............c
☐ Sharp-tailed Grouse...................................r............r............x

RAILS AND COOTS
☐ Virginia Rail ....r............r.............
☐ Sora* ....c............c ....c.............
☐ American Coot* ....o............o ....c ....r

CRANES
☐ Sandhill Crane* ....c............o ....c.............
☐ Whooping Crane.......................................r ....r.............r ....

PLOVERS AND SANDPIPERS
☐ Black-bellied Plover ....r...................r.............
☐ Lesser Golden-Plover ....x ....
☐ Semipalmated Plover ....r...................r.............
☐ Killdeer* ....o............c ....c ....o
☐ Mountain Plover ....x ....
☐ Black-necked Stilt ....x............x ....x.............
☐ American Avocet* ....o............o ....o ....
☐ Greater Yellowlegs....................................o............o ....o ....

Species	SP	SU	F	W
☐ Lesser Yellowlegs	o	o	o	
☐ Solitary Sandpiper	o	r	o	

PLOVERS AND SANDPIPERS CONTINUED

Species	SP	SU	F	W
☐ Willet*	o	r	o	
☐ Spotted Sandpiper*	c	c	c	
☐ Upland Sandpiper		x		
☐ Whimbrel	x			
☐ Long-billed Curlew*	o	o	o	
☐ Marbled Godwit	o	r	r	
☐ Red Knot	x		x	
☐ Sanderling	x	r	x	
☐ Semipalmated Sandpiper		r	o	
☐ Western Sandpiper	x	r	o	
☐ Least Sandpiper	o	r	o	
☐ Baird's Sandpiper	r	o	o	
☐ Pectoral Sandpiper			r	
☐ Dunlin	?	x		
☐ Stilt Sandpiper	r			
☐ Long-billed Dowitcher	o	o	o	
☐ Common Snipe*	c	c	c	o
☐ American Woodcock	?	?		

PHALAROPES

Species	SP	SU	F	W
☐ Wilson's Phalarope*		c	o	r
☐ Red-necked Phalarope		r	r	
☐ Red Phalarope		x		

JAEGERS

Species	SP	SU	F	W
☐ Parasitic Jaeger		x		

GULLS AND TERNS

Species	SP	SU	F	W
☐ Franklin's Gull	r	c	r	
☐ Bonaparte's Gull	o		r	
☐ Ring-billed Gull	o	o	o	
☐ California Gull	c	c	c	
☐ Western Gull			?	
☐ Sabine's Gull			x	
☐ Caspian Tern	r	o	o	
☐ Common Tern		r	r	
☐ Forster's Tern	o	o	o	
☐ Black Tern	o	o	o	
☐ Ancient Murrelet			x	

DOVES AND CUCKOOS

Species	SP	SU	F	W
☐ Rock Dove•	o	o	o	o
☐ Band-tailed Pigeon	x	x	?	?
☐ Mourning Dove*	o	o	o	x

☐ Black-billed Cuckoo ....r ....r...........r.............
☐ Yellow-billed Cuckoo..x ....x.............

OWLS
☐ Barn Owl..x.............
☐ Flammulated Owl...x.............
☐ Western Screech-Owl•. ....r ....r ....r.............r
☐ Great Horned Owl* ....c ....c ....c.............c
☐ Snowy Owl ....x........ x
☐ Northern Hawk Owl ....?.............
☐ Northern Pygmy-Owl• ....o...........o ....o ....r
☐ Burrowing Owl* ....r ....r............r.............
☐ Barred Owl ....x............x ....x...........x
☐ Great Gray Owl* ....o...........o ....o ....o
☐ Long-eared Owl* ....x............o ....o...........x
☐ Short-eared Owl* ....r ....o ....o ....r
☐ Boreal Owl*...o...........o ....o ....o
☐ Northern Saw-whet Owl* ....o...........o ....o ....o

NIGHTHAWKS
☐ Common Nighthawk* ....c...........c ....c............
☐ Common Poorwill* ....x...........x ....

SWIFTS AND HUMMINGBIRDS
☐ Black Swift..?.............
☐ Vaux's Swift ....?.............
☐ White-throated Swift ....x.............
☐ Blue-throated Hummingbird ....x...........x ....
☐ Magnificent Hummingbird ....x...........x ....
☐ Black-chinned Hummingbird ....r...........r.............
☐ Calliope Hummingbird*..........................c...........c ....c............
☐ Broad-tailed Hummingbird*.....................c...........c ....o............
☐ Rufous Hummingbird*..........................o...........c ....o............

KINGFISHERS
☐ Belted Kingfisher* ....c...........c ....c.........c

WOODPECKERS
☐ Lewis's Woodpecker*...............................o...........o ....r ....
☐ Red-headed Woodpecker ....x...........x ....
☐ Acorn Woodpecker................................x ....
☐ Red-naped Sapsucker...............................c...........c ....c.........x
☐ Williamson's Sapsucker* ....o...........o ....r............
☐ Downy Woodpecker* ....c...........c ....c.........c
☐ Hairy Woodpecker*..............................c...........c ....c.........c
☐ White-headed Woodpecker ....x...........x ....
☐ Three-toed Woodpecker*.......................o...........o ....r...........r
☐ Black-backed Woodpecker*......................r ....r..........r..........r

☐ Northern Flicker* ....c.............c...........c ....o
☐ Pileated Woodpecker.................................x......................

FLYCATCHERS
☐ Olive-sided Flycatcher*...................c............c...........c.............
☐ Western Wood-Pewee* ....c............c...........c.............
☐ Willow Flycatcher* ....c............c...........c.............
☐ Least Flycatcher ....o........................
☐ Hammond's Flycatcher ....o............o...........o ....
☐ Dusky Flycatcher*.............................c............c...........c.............
☐ Cordilleran Flycatcher•. ....c............c...........c.............
☐ Say's Phoebe ....r ....r............r ....
☐ Vermilion Flycatcher.........................x...........................
☐ Ash-throated Flycatcher ....x...........................
☐ Great Crested Flycatcher ....x..............
☐ Western Kingbird..........................r ....r............r ....
☐ Eastern Kingbird.............................o............o...........o ....
☐ Scissor-tailed Flycatcher...................x...........................

LARKS
☐ Horned Lark•. ....c............c...........c ....o

SWALLOWS
☐ Tree Swallow* ....a............a ....a............
☐ Violet-green Swallow*.......................c............c ....c............
☐ Northern Rough-winged Swallow* ....o............o ....o ....
☐ Bank Swallow*.................................c............c ....c............
☐ Cliff Swallow* ....a............a ....c.............
☐ Barn Swallow* ....c............c ....c.............

JAYS, MAGPIES AND CROWS
☐ Gray Jay*...c............c ....c...........c
☐ Steller's Jay* ....c............c ....c...........c
☐ Blue Jay..x x
☐ Pinyon Jay..x ....x...........x
☐ Clark's Nutcracker* ....c............c ....c...........c
☐ Black-billed Magpie* ....c............c ....c...........c
☐ American Crow* ....c............c ....c ....o
☐ Common Raven*...............................c............c ....c...........c

CHICKADEES
☐ Black-capped Chickadee* ....c............c ....c...........c
☐ Mountain Chickadee* ....c............c ....c...........c
☐ Plain Titmouse ....?.........................

NUTHATCHES
☐ Red-breasted Nuthatch* ....c............c ....c...........c

☐ White-breasted Nuthatch* ....c...........c ....c...........c
☐ Pygmy Nuthatch ....x.............

CREEPERS
☐ Brown Creeper* ....o............o ....o ....o

WRENS
☐ Rock Wren* ....o............o ....o ....o
☐ Canyon Wren...x ....x.........
☐ House Wren* ....c...........c ....c.............
☐ Winter Wren• ....x ....r..............? x
☐ Marsh Wren* ....c...........c ....c.............

DIPPERS
☐ American Dipper* ....c............c ....c...........c

KINGLETS AND GNATCATCHERS
☐ Golden-crowned Kinglet• ....o............o ....o ....r
☐ Ruby-crowned Kinglet* ....c............c ....o ....r
☐ Blue-gray Gnatcatcher ....x ....x.............

THRUSHES
☐ Western Bluebird ....o............r ....o ....
☐ Mountain Bluebird* ....c............c ....c............
☐ Townsend's Solitaire* ....c............c ....o ....o
☐ Veery• ....o............o ....o............
☐ Swainson's Thrush* ....c............c ....o ....
☐ Hermit Thrush* ....c............c ....o ....
☐ American Robin* ....a............a ....a ....r
☐ Varied Thrush....................................x............x ....x.............

MOCKINGBIRDS AND THRASHERS
☐ Gray Catbird• ....o............o ....r............
☐ Northern Mockingbird ....x ....x.............
☐ Sage Thrasher* ....c............c ....o ....
☐ Brown Thrasher ....x ....

PIPITS
☐ American Pipit• ....c............c ....c............?
☐ Sprague's Pipit ....x ....x.............

WAXWINGS
☐ Bohemian Waxwing ....o ....r.........o
☐ Cedar Waxwing ....o............o ....o ....o

SHRIKES
☐ Northern Shrike ....o ....o ....o
☐ Loggerhead Shrike• ....o ....r...........r.........o

STARLINGS
- ☐ European Starling* — c ... c ... c ... o

VIREOS
- ☐ Solitary Vireo — r ... r
- ☐ Warbling Vireo* — a ... a ... o
- ☐ Red-eyed Vireo — r ... r

WARBLERS
- ☐ Tennessee Warbler — x ... r ... x
- ☐ Orange-crowned Warbler• — o ... o ... o
- ☐ Nashville Warbler — x ... x
- ☐ Yellow Warbler* — a ... a ... c
- ☐ Chestnut-sided Warbler — x ... x
- ☐ Black-throated Blue Warbler — x
- ☐ Yellow-rumped Warbler* — a ... a ... c
- ☐ Townsend's Warbler — o ... o
- ☐ Blackburnian Warbler — x
- ☐ Palm Warbler — x
- ☐ Bay-breasted Warbler — x
- ☐ American Redstart — r ... r
- ☐ Prothonotary Warbler — x
- ☐ Northern Waterthrush — r ... r ... x
- ☐ MacGillivray's Warbler* — c ... c ... o
- ☐ Common Yellowthroat* — c ... c ... c
- ☐ Wilson's Warbler* — c ... c ... c
- ☐ Painted Redstart — ?
- ☐ Yellow-breasted Chat — x ... x ... x

TANAGERS
- ☐ Scarlet Tanager — x
- ☐ Western Tanager* — c ... c ... o

GROSBEAKS, BUNTINGS, SPARROWS, BLACKBIRDS, ORIOLES & FINCHES
- ☐ Rose-breasted Grosbeak — o
- ☐ Black-headed Grosbeak* — o ... c ... o
- ☐ Lazuli Bunting* — o ... o ... r
- ☐ Indigo Bunting — x ... x
- ☐ Dickcissel — x
- ☐ Green-tailed Towhee* — o ... c ... c
- ☐ Rufous-sided Towhee — r ... r ... r
- ☐ Canyon Towhee — x ... ?
- ☐ American Tree Sparrow — o ... o ... o
- ☐ Chipping Sparrow* — c ... c ... c ... ?
- ☐ Clay-colored Sparrow* — r
- ☐ Brewer's Sparrow* — c ... c ... c
- ☐ Vesper Sparrow — c ... c ... c

NO.	SPECIES	SP	SU	F	W
☐	Lark Sparrow	o	o	o	
☐	Black-throated Sparrow	x			
☐	Sage Sparrow	x	x		

GROSBEAKS, BUNTINGS, SPARROWS, BLACKBIRDS, ORIOLES & FINCHES CONTINUED

NO.	SPECIES	SP	SU	F	W
☐	Lark Bunting	r	r		
☐	Savannah Sparrow•	c	c	c	
☐	Grasshopper Sparrow		x		
☐	Fox Sparrow*	o	o	r	
☐	Song Sparrow*	c	c	c	o
☐	Lincoln's Sparrow*	o	c	c	
☐	Swamp Sparrow		?	?	
☐	White-throated Sparrow	r		r	
☐	White-crowned Sparrow*	a	a	a	r
☐	Harris's Sparrow	o		o	o
☐	Dark-eyed Junco*	a	a	c	o
☐	McCown's Longspur		x		
☐	Lapland Longspur	x			x
☐	Snow Bunting	x		r	o
☐	Bobolink*	o	o		
☐	Red-winged Blackbird*	c	c	c	o
☐	Western Meadowlark•	c	c	c	x
☐	Yellow-headed Blackbird*	c	c	c	x
☐	Rusty Blackbird			x	
☐	Brewer's Blackbird*	c	c	a	o
☐	Common Grackle*	c	c	c	
☐	Brown-headed Cowbird*	c	c	c	
☐	Orchard Oriole*	x			
☐	Northern Oriole*	o	o	o	
☐	Rosy Finch*	c	c	o	o
☐	Pine Grosbeak•	c	c	c	c
☐	Purple Finch				?
☐	Cassin's Finch*	c	c	c	o
☐	House Finch	x	x	x	x
☐	Red Crossbill*	o	o	o	o
☐	White-winged Crossbill*	x	x		x
☐	Common Redpoll	c		o	o
☐	Hoary Redpoll	x			x
☐	Pine Siskin*	c	c	c	o
☐	American Goldfinch*	c	c	c	o
☐	Evening Grosbeak*	c	o	c	c
☐	House Sparrow*	c	c	c	c

RECOMMENDED RESOURCES

Burt, William H. Grossenheider, Richard P. *A Peterson Field Guide to Mammals.* Houghton Mifflin Company.

Craighead, Frank C. *For Everything There Is A Season.* Falcon Press Publishers.

Craighead, John J. and Frank C. and Davis, Ray J. *A Peterson Field Guide to Rocky Mountain Wildflowers.* Houghton Mifflin Company.

Craighead, Karen. *Large Mammals of Yellowstone and Grand Teton National Parks.* Yellowstone Association for Natural Science, History and Education.

Larson, Leo L. *Grand Teton National Park Recreational Map.* Topographic, Waterproof and Non-waterproof. Contour Interval 80 feet.

Love, Dr. David and Reed, Dr. John. *Creation of the Teton Landscape.* Grand Teton Natural History Association.

Murie, Olaus J. *Animal Tracks.* Houghton Mifflin Company.

National Geographic. *Field Guide to the Birds of North America.* The National Geographic Society.

National Park Service. *Grand Teton, Official National Park Handbook.* Government Printing Office.

Olson, Linda L. and Bywater, Tim. *A Guide to Exploring Grand Teton National Park.* RNM Press.

Randall, Glenn. *The Modern Backpacker's Handbook.* Lyons and Burford Publishers.

Raynes, Bert and Wile, Darwin. *Finding the Birds of Jackson Hole.* Darwin Wile, Jackson, Wyoming.

Raynes, Bert. *Birds of Grand Teton National Park.* Grand Teton Natural History Association.

Shaw, Richard J. *Plants of Yellowstone and Grand Teton National Parks.* Wheelwright Press.

Stelfox, J. Brad and Lawrence, Lynn. *A Field Guide to the Hoofed Mammals of Jackson Hole.* Teton Science School.

Streubel, Donald. *Small Mammals of the Yellowstone Ecosystem.* Roberts Rinehart, Inc.

INDEX

Middle Fork of Granite Creek, 82
Middle Teton, 43
Miller Butte, 15
Mirror Lake, 92
Moose, 34, 45, 47, 49, 54, 68, 78, 120-121
Moose Basin, 116, 120-121
Moose Creek, 117, 119-120
Moose Entrance Station, 40, 45, 49, 54, 69, 74
Moose Ponds, 39, 46-47
Moose Village Store, 10
Moose Visitor Center, 4, 9-10, 43, 78, 83
Moose-Wilson Road, 68, 78, 83
Mount Moran, 13, 20, 49, 51-52, 59, 63, 65, 96-101, 104-105, 109, 112, 120
Moran Entrance Station, 96, 100, 105, 109, 112
Moran Junction, 20, 105
Mount Hunt Divide, 67, 86-88
Mount Leidy, 55, 98, 108
Mount Leidy Highlands, 55
Mount Meek Pass, 91-92
Mount Owen, 42, 55-56, 98
Mount Woodring, 51, 64
Mystic Island, 51, 98
National Elk Refuge, 11, 15
North Fork of Granite Canyon Trail, 53, 60-61, 64, 77, 82
North Fork of Granite Creek, 82
North Jenny Lake Junction, 45, 49
Open Canyon, 67-69, 80, 83-88
Open Canyon Creek, 87
Open Canyon Trail, 67-69, 80, 84-87
Open Canyon Trail Junction, 68, 80, 84-86
Owl Canyon, 116, 119-120
Owl Canyon Trail, 115
Owl Creek, 115-121
Owl Creek Loop, 115
Owl Creek Trail, 116, 118-119
Owl Peak, 119-120
Pacific Creek, 18, 104-105, 107-108
Pacific Creek Road, 105
Paintbrush Canyon, 39, 49-51, 53, 59, 63-65
Paintbrush Canyon To Paintbrush Divide, 39, 63
Paintbrush Canyon Trail, 49-50, 59, 64
Paintbrush Divide Trail, 64
Paintbrush Divide, 39, 53, 59, 63, 64, 65
Paintbrush-Cascade Canyon, 63
Phelps Lake, 5, 18, 20, 68-70, 83-86, 88-89, 113
Pilgrim Creek, 101, 106

NOTES

NOTES

NOTES

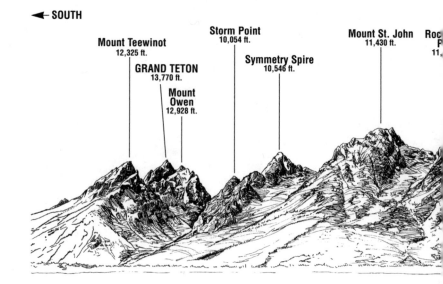

← SOUTH

Mount Teewinot
12,325 ft.

GRAND TETON
13,770 ft.

Mount
Owen
12,928 ft.

Storm Point
10,054 ft.

Symmetry Spire
10,546 ft.

Mount St. John
11,430 ft.

Roc
P
11,